THE PROCESS OF MODEL-BUILDING
IN THE BEHAVIORAL SCIENCES

The Process
of Model-Building
in the Behavioral Sciences

W. Ross Ashby

C. West Churchman

Harold Guetzkow

R. Duncan Luce

James G. March

William T. Morris

Ralph M. Stogdill, Editor

Ohio State University Press

Standard Book Number 8142-0136-9
Library of Congress Catalogue Card Number 74-93791
Printed in the United States of America
Copyright © 1970 by the Ohio State University Press
All Rights Reserved

"On the Art of Modeling," by William T. Morris
was originally published in *Management Science*
August, 1967, Vol. *13*, No. 12.
Reprinted by permission of the publisher.

Contents

99101

Foreword

I am pleased to have this opportunity to participate even in a minor way in this symposium. The topic is one which has intrigued me for some time in my own work, and I am particularly happy to note that while my attention has been diverted to other problems, we have reinstated the word "model" as opposed to that more exotic, but misunderstood word, "paradigm."

This conference exemplifies the strengths of a comprehensive university. The range of interests and disciplines represented by the sponsoring units is wide, yet can be brought into focus on a campus such as ours to deal with a complex and multi-disciplinary problem. The speakers bring with them varied backgrounds of training, university and departmental affiliations, and distinguished professional achievements.

As an administrator, I suppose I am—or should be—almost constantly in the process of mental model-building. While this process all too frequently is done in an inexact and unsophisticated manner by the day-to-day practitioner, it seems to me that it must be done, and must be done each day with more expertise.

I know of no topic that is more practical as our organizations, our missions, and our tools become more complex and as our expenditures—and consequently the expectations held for us—become larger and larger. I am not, therefore, merely welcoming you here to one more symposium, but am, instead, greeting you and your topic with enthusiasm and with high hopes.

As I understand the aims and mechanics of the symposium, the speakers were requested to address themselves to a common problem, but to approach it from different points of view. They were asked, not to develop a model, but to discuss the considerations that enter into the development of a model. This, then, is not expected to be a practical workshop on the methodology of model-building. Rather, it is an inquiry into, and an exploration of, the processing behaviors of the model builder. As the titles of the papers suggest, this inquiry will involve a variety of considerations.

Whereas considerable recent progress has been made in the development of models for solving practical problems, comparatively little attention has been devoted concurrently to the intellectual processes involved in model-building. It is hoped that this symposium will stimulate further inquiry into the problem.

John E. Corbally, Jr.

Acknowledgments

The papers in this book were presented at a symposium on The Process of Model-Building in the Behavioral Sciences, on April 20 and 21, 1967, at the Ohio State University. The Symposium Committee appreciates the support provided by the following sponsors: the Graduate School, the College of Administrative Science, the College of Education, the Mershon Foundation Social Science Program, the Department of Industrial Engineering, the Department of Psychiatry, and the Department of Psychology.

George S. Maccia
William T. Morris
James C. Naylor
Salomon Rettig
James A. Robinson
Ralph M. Stogdill
The Symposium Committee

THE PROCESS OF MODEL-BUILDING
IN THE BEHAVIORAL SCIENCES

Introduction:
The Student and Model-Building

This symposium is oriented toward the student rather than the practitioner. It is addressed indirectly to the large body of professors and scholars who attempt to teach the student how to build models. The symposium is not designed to teach model-building. It seeks rather to acquaint students with the discourse of several scholars who are masters of the art of dispelling the intellectual paralysis that many beginners experience when they are introduced to the literature on mathematical models.

The symposium had its origin in a concern for the problems encountered by the beginning student of model-building. He does not know where to begin, how to proceed, or where to end. A model as encountered in books and journals is usually presented as a *fait accompli*. The author seldom takes the reader into his confidence regarding the considerations that led to his formulation of the published model. As a consequence, the student remains almost completely in the dark regarding the author's starting points and the steps that he took to arrive at his chosen model. The student is often led unintentionally to believe that the problem is to discover one perfect model rather than to search for one or more models that may be useful for a given purpose.

The student of model-building seeks answers to several

questions that are not clarified by available textbooks. Among these are the following: How does one analyze a set of real events in order to isolate and define the important variables (dimensions) that appear to be operating? How does one determine the structure of relationships between the variables? Is intuition alone sufficient? Might the examination of empirical data aid in formulating the relationships? Given a fairly reliable idea about the content and structure of a system of events, how does one represent it in the form of a mathematical equation?

The foregoing questions are concerned with the methodology of model-building. Unfortunately for the student, no such methodology has been developed. In practice, the student finds that he must work at several different levels simultaneously. Objectively, he is confronted by the system of real events that he wants to analyze and describe. Subjectively, he is confronted by the problem of conceptualizing the real system in terms of variables and relationships that will be intellectually manageable, and that at the same time will constitute a valid representation of the real system. In addition, he must consider the problem of translating his conception of the system into a mathematical formula. If he wants to test the validity of his formula, he must also consider the problems of measurement and analysis of empirical data. The operations listed above require the application of varied abilities and skills. Professor Ashby's paper and the practical example discussed by Professor Morris should give insight into the considerations involved in analyzing a problem and translating it into a model. The program described by Professor March suggests that the task of learning model-building can be facilitated by demonstration, practice, and stimulating instruction. His work book in the Appendix should excite the imagination in suggesting that social events in great variety can be represented in the form of models.

It was with such considerations in mind that the Symposium Committee requested the speakers to address themselves to a common topic but to approach it from different points of view. It was thought that a varied approach might increase the likelihood of illuminating different levels and facets of the model-building process.

A study in the process of model-building can be regarded as a study in the intellectual activities of the model-builder. The model-builder is concerned with the description and explanation of a system of events in the real world. The investigation must be extended to include the model-builder's processing of information about the world of reality. When and where is such information obtained? When does such processing begin? Can we assume that it begins when the scientist first becomes aware of a problem as one that merits his thought and consideration? This is hardly a safe conclusion, since his very recognition of a problem is probably the result of a long background of training and experience, as Professor Guetzkow suggests.

It appears to be extremely difficult for the model-builder to maintain a high degree of sensitization to his own intellectual processes while at the same time trying to analyze and understand a system of external events. The gifted musician, writer, or artist may not be a good builder of mathematical models even though he is highly sensitized to his own thoughts and feelings, and can give them powerful artistic expression. He may not like to be bound by the same environmental constraints that limit the model-builder. Professor Guetzkow's observations suggest that when one's professional colleagues in face-to-face interaction provide conceptualizations, the process of defining an appropriate set of analytical concepts and of formulating the structure of a model can indeed cause stress. The individual approach involves less interpersonal stress, but deprives the model-builder of immediate criticisms and suggestions that might speed his progress.

The value of a client's participation in model-building is

confirmed by Professor Churchman's observations. We often forget that different valid models can be developed for the same set of real events. Engineers have developed different models for refining petroleum, brewing beer, and so on. That various methods may be valid and useful is evidenced by the wide consumer demand for different brands of the same product and by the large profits realized from their sale. The strucural and operational characteristics of a model are determined to a high degree by the purpose it is to serve. The client exercises a legitimate function in determining the characteristics of a model that is being developed for his use. Different models may be equally effective, but not equally practicable when evaluated in terms of the client's aims and resources.

Although a system of events can be conceptualized in different ways, not all are equally effective in yielding insight and understanding. Copernicus's view of the solar system as centered around the sun explained more than the previous view of a universe centered around the Earth. His discovery paved the way for Kepler's more accurate model, and for Newton's still more powerful explanatory model. Professor Ashby's paper illustrates the advantages that accrue when a wide range of knowledge from diverse sciences is brought to bear on a problem to effect an integration. Our ability to analyze a system of events to be modeled is limited by what we know, or rather do not know, about it. We may make useful speculations in the absence of sound knowledge, but accurate information is a help toward valid conceptualizations.

The development of models has been most successful in those areas of science that have access to precise measurement procedures. A system of measurement, once developed, may appear to be quite simple, self-evident, and ever-present. But this is not necessarily the case. Any system of measurement is a highly sophisticated human creation. It is usually preceded by a perception of the dimensions of reality that are required for accurate description of some set of events being observed. The usefulness and power of measurement increases with the development of precise and standardized scales for indicating degree or magnitude. But the accumulation of measurements and observations does not in itself generate a model. It is necessary for somebody to perceive structure in a mass of accumulated data in order to develop a model. It is at this stage particularly that a knowledge of mathematics is necessary for determining the structure of relationships that may exist in a highly complex set of data.

The physical sciences have an advantage by several centuries over the social sciences both in the conceptualization of the dimensions of the objective world that are relevant for observation, and in the development of precise instruments for measuring those dimensions. The physical sciences have the additional advantage of having defined those dimensions in terms that all scientists understand and accept. That is, the definition of a concept tends to mean the same thing to all physical scientists.

As indicated by Professor Luce, the social and behavioral sciences are confronted by a world of such seeming complexity that it is difficult to isolate a set of dimensions that adequately describe a set of events. Even for those dimensions that have been isolated, there is a tendency for scientists to disagree on how they should be defined. This means in effect that different social scientists may disagree on the basic characteristics of the dimension, although all may give it the same name. Such differences in conceptualization are reflected in research in that Scientist A may measure one characteristic of a complex concept while Scientist B may measure a different characteristic of the concept. Both may claim to have obtained measures on the same dimension, although their measures are not comparable. These considerations suggest that there is a need in the social and behavioral sciences for definitions of concepts that mean the same thing to all scientists as well as for standardized scales of measurement. These two basic conditions must be fulfilled in order for the concepts and research results of different scientists to be integrated into a single explanatory model.

It is difficult for the behavioral scientist to develop models for complete systems of events. As Professor Luce's paper indicates, our models tend to be restricted to small subsets of the systems that we seek to explain. If models are developed for several subsets of the same system, they can seldom be integrated. One reason for this inability is that the subsets may contain few, if any, variables in common. A second is that measurements in one subset may be made upon the actual variables that are involved, while in another subset measurements are made upon supposed correlates of the variables rather than upon the actual variables. Thus, the social scientist must deal with some of the same problems that confront the student of model-building. In order to develop good models, he must isolate the variables needed to account for the system to be explained and must, if possible, develop methods for measuring the actual variables rather than inferred correlates of the variables.

Another consideration concerns the criterion of creative work. There seems to be a tendency for behavioral scientists to evaluate creativity in terms of the invention of new names or definitions for well-known phenomena, and in terms of the construction of new measuring instruments. Faculty advisors sometimes refuse to approve a dissertation proposal that includes the use of standardized measuring devices. A student in the physical sciences is seldom required to reinvent the yardstick before being permitted to continue with his proposed research. The student in the behavioral sciences must deal not only with a complex world of social events; he is also compelled to deal with a fuzzy conceptualization and dimensionalization of the world he wants to study. His problem is further complicated by the unwillingness of his seniors to agree upon the definition of concepts, upon the use of standardized measuring instruments, and upon the value of data that are comparable from one study to another.

These issues are of direct relevance to model-building. We cannot claim to understand a set of events until we have acquired a model or theory that adequately accounts for the structural and operational characteristics of the system being observed. I am suggesting that when the student is a client, one of his purposes in using models might well be that of gaining insight and understanding. This purpose does not preclude his use of models for solving practical problems. In either event, he needs to realize that he is dealing not only with an opaque social world, but with a body of conceputalizations that is less than adequate for his purposes. Great opportunities and challenges await the student in the behavioral sciences. We shall no doubt need Keplers who are capable of perceiving structure in large masses of accumulated data before any behavioral Newtons or Einsteins emerge. However, if Professor March's program for teaching creative model-building gains wide acceptance, it may be possible to short-cut the route to powerful analytical concepts and systems.

The discussion thus far suggests that the student of model-building needs to become the master of several skills. He needs skill in observing and analyzing a system of real events in order to isolate the determining variables that are operating in the system. He needs to define each variable or dimension in terms that will permit other students to identify exactly the same dimension. He needs skill in perceiving or determining the relationships between the different dimensions. That is, he needs not only to determine the structural components of a system, but its operational characteristics as well. His conceptualization, consisting of a set of defined concepts and a set of statements about the relationships between the concepts, constitutes his model of the system.

A student's analysis of a system may be based upon direct observation of the system at work or upon a set of measurements made upon relevant dimensions of the system. If the system is highly complex, he will probably need to resort to measurement. Having obtained a set of measurements, he examines it in relation to his model to answer the question, "Are the measurements related as hypothesized by the model?" In order to perform this test, the student needs skill in measurement, mathematics, and research design.

There is a school of thought in the behavioral sciences which maintains that premature hypothesizing and model-building may close the door to further inquiry. This school prefers to analyze and reanalyze data on a trial and error basis until a formula is found that fits the data. I would maintain that trial and error procedure is based on a tentative hypothesis regarding the possible relationships in a set of data. If so, an explicit statement of the hypothesis is not a handicap. If data from repeated measurements on a system fail to fit a given model, common sense dictates the development of a better model as a guide to further research. After all, the only knowledge we have in science is that which comes to us in the form of a model or theory, whether or not it is labeled as such.

Outlining what one ought to do does not necessarily tell one how to do what ought to be done. Professors March and Morris are particularly aware of the viewpoint of the student who might like a set of specific instructions for developing a model. I must state, however, that it was not the purpose of this symposium to set forth any cookbook procedures for developing models. Its purpose, rather, was to examine the process of model-building in the hope of making explicit the nature of the intellectual operations and requisite skills involved. This is by no means an easy task.

Scientific method and the philosophy of science, developed to a high degree of sophistication, are concerned with the testing of theories. They tell us little or nothing about the development of theories. A model, as conceived by the authors of this symposium, exhibits all the logical and empirical characteristics of a theory. The term *model* may be regarded as an unpretentious name for a theory. Perhaps the term *model* also implies the probability of a somewhat shorter life span than that hoped for a theory. In any event, model-building and theory-building involve creative intellectual operations.

Too little is known about the nature of the creative process. Current research on creativity has succeeded in identifying some personality and intellectual characteristics of the creative individual. But knowledge of the characteristics of the creative person is not identical with knowledge of the creative process. It was the hope of the committee and of its sponsors that one of the outcomes of this symposium might be the definition of a problem area and a focusing of attention upon the problem as one that merits intensive investigation. We need in particular more autobiographical studies of model-building projects by scientists who are sensitive to their own intellectual operations, to the sources of their concepts, to alternative formulations of relationships, and to the steps of reasoning that lead to a finished model. It is to be hoped that the future autobiographer of a modeling project will be able to set forth detailed answers to questions such as the following:

Why were the variables selected for the model?

Why were other possibly relevant variables omitted?

Why was the specific set of relationships between variables postulated for the model?

What other relationships might have been hypothesized?

Are the variables assumed to be complex or unitary?

If some of the variables are complex in structure, is it assumed that the components interact to produce an averaging out effect?

To what extent does the model appear to describe the set of events in the real world that it was designed to explain?

The symposium is addressed to the teacher as well as to the student. The teacher, as a result of natural inclination, practice and centuries of tradition, has become oriented toward the end product (the model). The student, however, tends to be oriented toward the processes that are involved in model-building. The teacher, when he says, "Here is a model that I have developed for you," tends to become impatient with the student who does not immediately comprehend all that is involved in the model. The student seldom has the courage to ask, "How did you arrive at the model?" But that is what he would like to know.

The symposium is also addressed to the researchers who are investigating creativity. It is hoped that the papers will define and open up a field of research in which the creative scientist will serve as the subject of investigation. The inquiry should be concerned, not with the traits of the scientist, but with his intellectual (subjective) operations and processes that result in specific creative achievements. Hopefully, the results of such research will tell the student more than we are now able to tell him about the methods of model-building.

An attempt has been made to relate the aims of the symposium to a framework of topics that the following papers will analyze in detail. It has seemed desirable to take cognizance of the fact that the present interest in model-building (as well as the problem of model-building itself) is anchored in the wider cultural environment, and is particularly indicative of the state of the social and behavioral sciences. None of the papers overstates our achievements in attempting to explain the real world in terms of models. This open recognition of the present state of the behavioral sciences is not necessarily an indication of pessimism regarding their possibilities for future development. It is rather a conscious avowal of the need and hope for more adequate conceptualizations of the real world and for models that have demonstrable descriptive and predictive powers.

The Client and the Model

In this paper[1] I shall be reviewing a series of thoughts that I have had on the subject of the "client" and his relationship to scientific endeavor. I shall be talking about theory for the sake of someone rather than theory for the sake of truth in the abstract.

By way of background it seems safe to say that the notion that theoretical constructs are developed for the sake of someone is not a new notion at all. Many men in history, for example Kepler, ardently believed that the constructs of the human mind were for the glorification of God. In this case the "client" is someone far superior to the theorizer.

On the other hand, there have also been a number of distinguished people who have believed that theory is for the sake of helping someone inferior to themselves in some regard. This notion of the "client" is certainly close to the dictionary concept because the term client itself derives from the idea of "leaning upon" and the first definition the *Oxford Dictionary* offers is one in which the client is a dependent. In this mode the theorizer is the "expert" who assists the client in ways that the client is not capable of assisting himself. The theorizer might be an economist or a medical practitioner or an engi-

---

1. This research was supported in part by the National Aeronautics and Space Administration under General Grant #NSG-243-62 under the University of California.

neer. In any of these instances the expert is judged to have knowledge that the client lacks. The relationship between the theorizer and the client is a very simple one. In our free society the client may, if he wishes, pay the expert so much to answer questions that are of interest to the client. The expert's task is to answer the questions as truthfully as he can, using his own factual and theoretical knowledge.

But there is another role that the "client" can play with respect to theorizing and model-building and it is that role that I wish to examine in this paper. The role arises from the philosophical thought that the real test of the meaning of a theory and of its validity lies in what the "client" does with it. Again it is an old thought but in modern times has been expressed most emphatically by the philosophical school we call pragmatism. Pragmatism in its vaguer forms states that truth is what works out, i.e., that a theoretical construct has meaning and validity provided that it becomes meaningful to someone and assists him in attaining what he wishes in a successful way. Under the terms of this definition, the client becomes a very essential part of the whole methodology of model-building. One cannot merely state that the theory or model is valid provided it tests successfully against "experience"; rather, it must test successfully against an experience that is oriented toward a purpose. The test of the model lies in whether the model can be used in accomplishing the client's purposes.

Even so, at the outset there does not seem to be any great difficulty facing us in terms of using the client as a standard for the model. Apparently all we need to do is determine what it is that the client wishes to accomplish. Once this determination is made we develop a model of his environment in which his purposes can be most successfully accomplished by means of various kinds of designs. After we have finished our task of model-building all we need now to do is to determine whether or not the client's purposes were successfully accomplished by means of the application of the model. Something like this way of phrasing the problem is certainly what I found when I began reading the literature of the pragmatists.

Of course it was easy for me to see that there were some serious objections to this account. For one thing it seemed to me to be rather deficient if one were trying to claim that the *ultimate* test of model-building was to be found in this kind of process. One implication of the argument is that the "truth" of a theory must depend entirely on the purposes and the intelligence of the "client" so that a theory might be true for one individual and not true for another, or for one culture and not for another, and so on. This is old-fashioned relativism, a doctrine that is intolerable to the philosophical mind because it is completely unreflective. It cannot ask itself whether or not its own view of the matter is a valid one, because if it does then it needs to find a client for whom the relativistic doctrine is useful, so that relativism becomes a form of relativism, and so on. Relativism is only relativistically true.

But I don't want to pursue the philosophical paradox of the relativistic doctrine of the client. Instead it seemed to me some twenty years ago when I began thinking about this matter in some depth that the procedure outlined above is deficient because it glides over some very critical issues: *who* is the client, *what* does the client want, and *how* do we determine whether he has "satisfactorily" attained what he wants.

Two early experiences shook whatever confidence I might have had in the rather easy manner in which Dewey and James tried to handle the problem of the client in pragmatism. During the war I posed as a statistician and attempted to assist research workers in applying statistical methods in the analysis of their data. I also tried to develop some sound statistical procedures for the inspection of army ordnance materiel. In both cases it seemed very evident to me that the ways in which the researchers and the inspectors were pursuing their goals could be vastly improved by a bit of statistical model-building. In those days, analytical chemists would take six readings for an analysis and automatically throw away the most deviant. It was a bit like a family, after having had six children, deciding that the only thing to do was to throw away the worst of the lot. The need for some model that justified the throwing away of an observation and developing an estimation procedure on the basis of the model seemed quite clear to me. I think I must have actually believed that all that was required was to sit down and talk sensibly to the chemist, showing him that there was a far more reasonable procedure that is grounded in statistical theory. I also discovered that in the laboratory where I worked no physicist would ever dream of using any modern statistical models for the analysis of his data. Instead he simply looked at the averages and made his own judgment. True, he often calculated the probable error, but only to perform a kind of scientific ritual that was followed by his forefathers and therefore seemed suitable for his own generation.

In the area of inspection, however, the situation seemed far more serious although not necessarily any more irrational. I found that small arms ammunition was being tested by taking a sample of 100 primers and subjecting them to a standard blow. If they all went off then the lot was considered acceptable. If one failed then 200 were inspected by the same procedure and if all of these passed the lot was accepted. A bit of model building showed quite clearly that the probability of accepting a lot with say 1 per cent or even up to 5 per cent defective items was not very low. Hence if the procedure then being used were applied to a lot of low quality, one could expect an alarming number of misfires in the field.

What happened? Did the analytic chemist smile with joy when I presented him a rational model for discarding observation? Did the physicist leap at the opportunity of employing rigorous statistical methods in the analysis of his data? Did those in charge of the inspection of army materiel respond immediately when a more rational plan for inspection was presented to them? Of course not. I began to get my first real glimpse of what the client was like and what his "purposes" really were. It was quite evident that in all three cases the individuals involved were greatly influenced by a conservative philosophy. It was their feeling that unless they clearly saw the need for change and the reasons why the change constituted an improvement they were unlikely to even pay attention to what was being suggested. Since to understand what I was recommending required some of their time, they did an unconscious bit of calculation and decided that the time required was not worth it.

At this point the classical pragmatist might say that the statistical models simply did not "work out" in practice, no matter how elegant and rational they may have appeared to the statistician. This answer might have sufficed in the case of the physicist working on a piece of basic research or even for the analytic chemist, despite the fact that in both cases the "optimum" strategy was not being followed. Indeed one physicist pointed out to me that there was no need for refined statistical techniques in physical experimentation since the physicist had plenty of time, money, and slave labor to collect as much data as he wanted. If there was ever any doubt about the results he could just go ahead and collect a lot more information.

But in the area of inspection the case is somewhat different. Indeed I began to get the first serious glimmer of the problem of the identification of the client. Certainly it would have been a mistake to say that an inspector at one of the ammunition plants was the "client," nor would it have been correct to say that the army administrators were the clients. In fact the only safe statement one could make about membership in the "set of clients" was that the soldier in the field was clearly a member of this set. And I supposed to myself that if the soldier in the field were asked if he minded having ammunition that was 5 per cent defective I could well imagine what his answer would be.

After a great deal of effort and time we were able to install more rational inspection procedures, and we were able to convince the analytic chemists to use "Student t-tests" and more rational methods of discarding observations. The physicists, in their affluent society, don't really matter in this story.

The subsequent story of the analytic chemists and the inspectors has an important moral. In both cases the procedures we recommended replaced those then in practice, but then followed an institutionalization of our recommendations. I dare say today that if someone came along in analytic chemistry or in ammunition inspection and tried to suggest an improvement over the procedures we installed, the clients would again resist the new recommendations.

Thus we come to a far deeper and much more significant view of the relationship of the client to the model. It is no longer appropriate to say that the client comes to the model-builders, states his question, and then the model-builder develops an optimal or better procedure and passes the recommendation back to the client. Nor is it appropriate to say that the "test" of the model lies in whether the client successfully uses the recommendations in the pursuit of his goals. Instead we must now realize that there are a number of strategies which the model builder may follow in "selling" or "persuading" the client. If a model-builder simply waits around to see whether the client uses his recommendations, then this is one strategy and in my experience not a particularly good one. If the model-builder, using whatever techniques he can, tries to brief the client and to persuade him that the recommendations are reasonable, then this is another strategy, and in my experience may sometimes be successful. It turns out to be more successful if the model-builder is well aware of the politics that are required in order to get the attention of the client and to get him to understand what is being said to him. Hence we must say that the "test" of the model in terms of the client's activities depends in part at least upon the strategy of the model-builder in developing his relationships with the client. It begins to look as though the model-builder must "sweep in" the characteristics of the client into his model.

The point is well brought out in the many experiences of operations research in its efforts to bring into reality the recommendations that are inherent in OR models. Time and time again a client is indifferent to or feels he has justifiable reasons for rejecting the recommendations made by the OR team after long and intensive study.

Well, then, suppose we do examine the client and ask ourselves what we can learn about him in order to develop an optimal strategy for the implementation of our model. This was very much the point of view that I had in the late forties when I began to become intensely interested in the psychological and sociological aspects of human personality. It was my feeling that it would be possible so to describe an individual that one could precisely define the conditions under which he would respond to various environmental stimuli.

But when I examined the psychological and sociological literature, I found that despite a growing literature describing many, many aspects of the human individual, not a single item of this literature seemed applicable to the problem at hand. It was impossible to find in psychological and sociological ar-

ticles and books any clear indication of how one should proceed in attempting to get the client to recognize the importance of recommendations or to get him into the position of
doing something about it. Of course there was some literature
in marketing and sociology on persuasion, but this literature
seemed more interested in the attempt to sell an item than an
idea. Furthermore, the studies of personality, attitude, and
opinion seemed to many of us to be less than satisfactory because they were couched in a language that was difficult to
interpret in terms of a "client" of the model-builder.

The very natural thing to do, therefore, was to develop
one's own language which would fit into the language of decision-making models most adequately. Since decision-making models essentially look at a decision-maker as someone
faced with a set of alternative choices of action with a specific
set of objectives, then why not attempt so to describe the personality of a human being in these terms? Thus it seemed
quite reasonable to say that the personality of a human being
represents the typical ways in which he responds to his environment in order to accomplish his goals. In our study on
"Psychologistics" [1], Russell Ackoff and I set forth to provide
a basic framework for human personality as well as "social
group" in terms of these basic elements: the probability of
choice of the decision-maker, the behavior patterns available
to him, and the characteristics of his environment. We
thought we had succeeded reasonably well in defining such
obscure concepts as knowledge, intention or value of ends,
attitudes and traits, as well as various sociological measures.
We believed we had developed a method of describing a client which could on the one hand make full use of the literature in psychology and sociology that was relevant and on
the other hand would enable us to understand how one should
proceed in the specific case of a client faced with a set of rec-

ommendations. We were by no means the only people interested in trying to characterize the client more precisely. In fact the whole development of measurement of utilities could be looked upon as a similar effort in which the researcher is attempting to come much closer to grips with the problem of measuring the values of the client.

In the 1940's we entered into this activity with a great deal more optimism than any of us have twenty years later. Perhaps we were naïve in thinking that the psychologists and sociologists would have a strong interest in "reducing" their concepts to some base that could be incorporated within mathematical decision-making models.

Perhaps, too, we were much too optimistic in terms of our abilities to measure the properties that we had so carefully defined. For example, if one attempts to apply some of the theory of the measurement of utilities in practical cases one finds almost insuperable obstacles. The kind of choices which we must observe in order to assess a decision-maker's values for various objectives are simply impossible to construct in any realistic way. For example, if an organization wishes in addition to maximizing profits to have due regard for the interest of the public, for its own personnel, and so on, then a list of objectives is generated for the client. The problem is to translate this list into a set of numbers which can form the basis of our calculations of optimal strategies for the client. In order to apply utility theory, however, one generally has to present the client with what are called "gambles," and the attempt to apply this notion in any realistic situation gets to be very silly indeed. It was for this reason that Ackoff and myself tried to develop what we called an "approximate measure of value" which would be both practical and interpretable by the model-builder. Back of our technique, in other words, was an explicit and well defined notion of the value of an objective. The technique does require the client to make a number of judgments, sometimes called "subjective" judgments by those who naïvely believe that there are *any* objective judgments to be found in this world!

It began to look as though the program we envisaged in the 1940's was an enormous one and that we had hardly scratched the surface of our understanding of the client. One of the things that we did not delve into deeply in "Psychologistics," nor did others like us in economics consider it, was the whole problem of the politics of organizations. This aspect of decision-making represents the loyalties and antagonisms, the coalitions and disillusions of the various sub-groups of an organization, their power structure, their means of attempting to close out certain efforts, and the general means by which certain groups attain leadership. At the present time we have no notion of how to make the political structure of an organization so explicit that its description can assist us in developing our strategies vis à vis the client.

I still think our earlier program was a sensible one and we have some reason to expect that in time to come the wealth of literature in psychology and sociology will be available to guide the model-builder in his relationships with the client.

But there are some problems that the literature itself has never considered and these today form the background of most of my interest in the problem of this paper.

The first is the identification of a client, the problem that I mentioned briefly and that now needs to be considered in greater detail. As I was saying earlier, we had set about trying to describe a client in terms of his alternative behavior patterns, his environment, etc. All of this effort, and indeed all of utility theory, presupposes that we can identify *who* the client is, i.e., that we can point to a person and say: "*that* individual is the client." Anyone who has worked in decision-making organizations, however, knows that it is not easy at all to tell who the client is. The first inclination is to identify the client with the people who have "top responsibility" for the operation of the organization, the so-called top managers. But it's obvious both in terms of feasibility and also in terms of politics that top managers are not the only decision-makers, or may not be decision-makers at all in many instances. The objectives and constraints on any individual or subgroup of an organization depend on the decisions and attitudes of many other people in the organization. One rather simple-minded way of defining a decision-maker in an organization is to say that X is a decision-maker if when X is persuaded about the correctness of a course of action the entire organization will implement it. This X rarely is a single individual, and may not be identifiable by any existing organizational label like "chief executive officer."

We should note that the decision-maker and the client need not be the same. The client is the individual (or group) who is the standard of performance of the system: his is the interest that is to be served. If a decision-maker does not serve his interest, then the decision-maker is wrong. The correct decision-maker is therefore a problem of design.

Whatever may be the difficulties of identifying decision-makers in industrial firms, these difficulties become even greater when we proceed to what is probably a much more important type of operations research activity, namely the development of models for government agencies. Here the nature of the decision-maker becomes very obscure. I know of one project where twenty separate government agencies are involved in decisions about how to take off waste water from a rich farming area. In this instance it is obviously impossible to point to any individual or any agency or subset of the total class agencies which represent *the* decision-maker.

Furthermore, even if we could say that some group of agencies is the decision-maker, we would have to decide whether the group ought to be in terms of the interests of the ultimate "client," the public. I remember back in the 1940's when we were working with the City Planning Commission of Philadelphia on a problem concerned with slums in South Philadelphia. We soon found ourselves asking who the decision-maker should be: City Hall, or the people in the area, or what? The sociologist in the City Planning Commission told us that all our worries were vapors. For him it was quite clear that the ward leaders in the South Philadelphia area knew the values of the people in the area and could safely be regarded as the decision-makers. Apparently he saw no reason to question whether the ward leaders were the proper decision-makers for the public.

This is a very curious situation indeed. Here we have a number of models to describe optimal behavior for decision-makers under various kinds of conditions. If we are to apply these models we obviously need to point out who the decision-maker and the client really are. But we have no model that helps us to identify such individuals. We have no clearcut guides that tell us what we need to examine in an organization in order to identify them. Our typical mode of procedure is to make a guess that certain people in various key positions have a say about what happens in the organization. We then develop a working hypothesis that these individuals constitute the decision-maker. We try out our ideas on them and see what kinds of repercussions occur throughout the organization. If the reactions of other parts of the organization indicate that we have not found our X then we enlarge the number of people and also perhaps add additional properties in order to set up a second working hypothesis about the decision-maker. The trouble with this kind of ad hoc procedure is that many of the steps we take may be irreversible. I know of one famous study where the operations research team assumed that top management was the decision-maker and, except for keeping middle management informed, largely ignored the attitudes of the middle managers. It so happened in this case the middle managers were the ones who had to implement the recommendations of the OR team. The middle managers had the attitude that their positions were threatened by the OR recommendation, which in effect meant automating a very significant part of the middle management decision-making. Since middle management controlled the implementation, it was not surprising that the recommendation fell flat on its face after one year of its operation. Here the OR team had failed to identify the decision-maker, to be sure, but it was not given an opportunity to revise its estimate and set up a second working hypothesis.

I'm not sure, too, that this whole method of approach doesn't miss the point. Is it even proper to go into an organization and by listening and looking around a bit, try to make a decision as to "who is responsible"? Such a procedure does not necessarily lead us to the *correct* decision-maker. Even if we identify the X which can implement a decision once X is convinced, how can we be so sure that we have really optimized? Perhaps the X that we are talking about operates with the wrong objectives relative to the client. The correct decision-maker is that group of people who ought to make the decisions of the firm, not those who actually do. If we develop a model for an organization and look at the existing decision-maker and optimize for him, may we not be running the risk of optimizing for exactly the wrong reason?

This question has a still more general form that deals with the whole relationship between reality and the model. All along we have been assuming that the client is a real entity out there whose life is independent of the model. The model-builder as we have been describing him is someone who "looks at" the client and decision-maker, and then looks at the results once a recommendation has been made. But what has been said above implies that the decision-maker and client now become a part of the model, i.e., a part of the life of the model-builder. What's happened to reality then? What is it that "gives" us information about the real situation? Well, we could say that our observations supply us with the fundamental data that we then put into the model much as we put information into a computer. The data are usually assembled in order to estimate the coefficients of the model. But now, what I've just been saying indicates a great difficulty in this procedure. I have just been saying that the point is not to identify who the decision-maker is but who he should be, because otherwise we may very well be working for precisely the wrong decision-maker. The ordnance managers during the war might be quite satisfied with a certain level of quality in order to expedite their logistical problems. But since the soldier in the field is the "client," the ordnance managers may have been the wrong decision-makers.

But if the problem is not what is but what ought to be, then how does observation help us to solve the problem? The ought-to-be lies within the model, because our models develop optimal strategies and have the language that permits them to make assertions in the optative mood. In effect the maximum of a function subject to constraints is a mathematical assertion that can be translated into the assertion that the decision-maker ought to do certain things. But isn't it true that the observations of reality are in the indicative mood? They supposedly tell us what is the case, or will be, or has been. Do they also tell us what ought to be the case?

This is a very fascinating problem from a philosopher's

point of view. The question is now, "How can anyone interested in developing models for clients use observations in order to support the recommendation that he makes to the clients?" This is another reason why Dewey's "works out" criterion gets us into difficulties, because we need to ask: works out for whom? and is it proper that it work out for one individual but not for another?

A little reflection, however, does convince us that the problem so stated need not be insoluble. Positivism, to be sure, has argued that the observations of a human being can be translated into sentences which are in the indicative mood. Positivism has never made any sincere attempt to establish the correctness of this doctrine and indeed there seems to be good reason to say that the so-called data of human experience are not in the indicative mood at all. If we are observing certain things about the world, we come to a judgment about what is happening in the environment about us, and as we turn to our fellow men in this judgment we are asking them, first, whether their judgments are in accord with our own and, second, if sufficient agreement occurs, we are asking that the data be accepted. In fact, we are saying that the data elements of a data bank are really themselves instructions. The data are to be accepted under certain conditions. The authorization for accepting the data lies within a certain kind of management system within each organization. This management system says in effect which data are to be used and under what conditions. Its statements are therefore in the imperative mood. Since they are, one can reasonably ask whether the data management system is operating correctly. One can in fact build a model of the data management system and talk about optimal utilization of information in organizations.

As a consequence it does not seem impossible to put the two problems of developing recommendations for managers and the use of data in our models into one package, but the package begins to look very large and cumbersome. We are now, I think, faced with the problem of how we can begin to integrate the pieces of model-building that have taken place in the last two decades. On the one hand, we have models that describe various kinds of operations of organizations, e.g., inventory systems, transportation systems, educational systems, and so on. Secondly, we have models that describe decision-makers, their alternative choices, their environment, their attitudes, their values, and so on. Third, we have models that describe information systems: how data is collected, how it is stored, how it is retrieved, how it is interpreted, and so on. What we lack at the present time is any way to integrate these three components of the model-client problem. In the academic field one finds people working in one of the three sectors: modeling of systems, modeling of people and social groups, and modeling of information systems. We still lack any clear way of how to bring together these various sectors of effort.

I wish I could end this paper by saying that I had found the correct way and that I could lay out the details of it in an exact set of specifications. I haven't, but I consider the problem to be the most serious one we face today in the methodology of model construction, whenever we take the attitude that theory is for the sake of some client.

The problem, to recapitulate, is this: how can we develop a model which will assure us that a certain way of modeling a system *and* of selecting the decision-maker and client of the system *and* of using evidence in support of our recommendations are all optimal; or if not optimal, at least better than some other method?

BIBLIOGRAPHICAL NOTE

1. An early attempt to classify theories of evidence and to point out the strengths and weaknesses of each was my *Theory of Experimental Inference* (New York: Macmillan, 1948), largely influenced by the work of E. A. Singer, Jr., later published in his *Experience and Reflection* (Philadelphia: University of Pennsylvania Press, 1959).

2. The attempt to define psychological and sociological concepts in decision-making terms was first made by Russell L. Ackoff and myself in "Psychologistics," mimeographed (Philadelphia: University of Pennsylvania, 1946). Subsequently the ideas of this book were re-examined and amplified in our *Methods of Inquiry* (New York: Educational Publishers, 1950), in my *Prediction and Optimal Decision* (New York: Prentice Hall, 1961), and in Ackoff's *Design of Social Research* (Chicago: University of Chicago Press, 1963).

3. Three works of mine summarize the concerns described at the end of this essay:

    Challenge to Reason (New York: McGraw-Hill Book Co., 1968), says that since we have no adequate method of understanding the whole system, social systems tend to take on an ethics of their own.

    The Systems Approach (New York: Delacorte Press, 1968), describes and criticizes various efforts now being conducted under this label.

    Design of Inquiring Systems (in preparation) is an on-going study of our capability of designing systems that can conduct inquiry for specific purposes; it is an attempt to model the strategies of the inquirer. Six chapters have been completed which are a part of the Working Paper Series of the Social Sciences Laboratory, University of California, Berkeley.

CHAPTER THREE

BY HAROLD GUETZKOW

A Decade of Life with the
Inter-Nation Simulation

This autobiographical essay[1] describes the influences of milieux on the development of a model in international relations, the "Inter-Nation Simulation," and the methodology used in its construction. During the past ten years it has been my privilege to nurture the growth of this "first generation effort" toward eventual realization of an operating model of our world community. The Inter-Nation Simulation is the outcome of a great complex of influences, not the least of which was my good fortune to live in a society where resources for scholarly work were available through academic establishments, generously undergirded by support from private foundations and government funds.[2]

---

1. The writing of this essay was made possible by the author's occupancy of the Gordon Scott Fulcher Chair of Decision-Making at Northwestern University, complemented with funds from the Carnegie Corporation of New York.

2. My gratitude is unbounded for a decade of opportunities to pursue international relations research with risk as to "pay-off." My seminal stay during 1956-67 at the Center for Advanced Study in the Behavioral Sciences in Stanford was financed by the Ford Foundation. Exploratory runs of the Inter-Nation Simulation were underwritten in 1957-59 by funds from the Carnegie Corporation of New York. During 1959-63 the research was supported by the Behavioral Sciences Division of the U. S. Air Force Office of Scientific Research (Contract No. AF49(638)-742 and Grant No. AF-AFOSR 62-63). During this period special tasks were undertaken for Project Michelson of

Let me briefly describe the Inter-Nation Simulation before delineating the ways in which the milieux influenced its development. By assembling two to five persons in a quasi-bureaucratic team, one has "decision makers" for a "nation." By placing varying constraints upon their decision-making, the political, economic, and military characteristics of their nation may be differentiated from those of other nations. The decision-makers are responsible for both the internal and external affairs of their governments. Through a set of programs some of the consequences of their decisions may be computed; these outputs along with the non-programmed consequences of actions then constitute the bases for decisions taken in the next round of activity. By composing an "international system" of some five to nine such simulated nations, a world in miniature is constructed. Permit some of the participants to serve as representatives in an "international organization"; establish "news media" as well as "world statistical services," so that the direct interactions among the nations are complemented through these sources of information. One then has an operating "international system," a more detailed description of which is given in our "Simulation in International Relations" [17].

This retrospective essay will focus on the substantive and methodological decisions that emerged from the intellectual and social milieux provided by the persons and institutions who most influenced me during the initial development of the simulation. Let me first describe these milieux, so that their impact on the realization of the Inter-Nation Simulation may be chronicled.

The plan for the development of the Inter-Nation Simula-

the Department of Navy (N1 23 (60530) 25875A). After 1964 the work was financed by a contract from the Advanced Research Projects Agency (SD 260) of the U. S. Department of Defense, with funds from the Carnegie Corporation of New York more recently providing for its direction.

tion took its form during a year spent at the Center for Advanced Study in the Behavioral Sciences, 1956-57. At the time of my arrival in Palo Alto, my thinking as a social scientist was anchored in a web of three intellectual commitments:

To the generation of knowledge for immediate application, especially with respect to the problems of peace and war

To problem-oriented research that is multi-disciplinary

To the development of an experimental social science, building eclectically in a cumulative way

Consider the implications of each of these commitments for research in international relations:

In developing fundamental knowledge to apply to the problems of peace and war, it was assumed that research efforts should encompass many aspects of international relations, for practical problems come in "wholes." The political exercises which Hans Speier talked about at the Center and which were based on work at the RAND Corporation [11] seemed constricted in being crisis-oriented. The tradition of war-gaming tended to be tactical in outlook. Yet one could build thereon, despite such narrowness of scope.

If the research were to be problem-oriented, it would need to be supplemented by whatever disciplines might contribute. It was taken for granted that my work in international relations would certainly encompass the individual level, leaning heavily upon the contributions of many in decision-making; the presence of Richard Snyder at the Center reinforced this orientation [45]. It was clear that the research would utilize the results of our knowledge about groups—be they face-to-face, organizational, or societal in their inclusiveness—given my interests after six years of work with Herbert Simon [27]. A small seminar at the Center at Stanford included Charles McClelland [29]; the vigor of his presentations showing the relevance of systems theory reinforced my willingness to use whatever capabilities were available from within all the social sciences.

It was a foregone conclusion that I would build eclectically upon what had gone before and would be integrative with respect to the work of others in international affairs. I found it easy at the Center to lean upon other seminar members interested in international relations, namely Karl Deutsch [8] and Wilbur Schramm [37]. With the Stanford University Library at hand, it was possible to dig deeply into the writings of others, including the contributions that Raymond Cattell [5] already had made to the study of the dimensions of nations.

These were the "initial conditions" of my milieux. These background commitments were reinforced by my peers at the Center. The alternative of researching broadly within empirical materials per se in the tradition of the behavioral scientist seemed impractical at the time, considering problems of access to affairs of nation-states. The development of a political-economic-military simulation involving both men and programs appealed to me as an experimental vehicle which might have a scope adequate to meet my interests in application. Here was a medium in which a broadly engaged social scientist might sketch, dipping eclectically into the various disciplines as the study of policy problems might require. With notes jumbled in my briefcase I left the Center in the summer of 1957 to begin a new life in the study of international relations at Northwestern University, where work on the Inter-Nation Simulation was continued.

Formation of the Simulation

In the early years of Northwestern's Program of Graduate Training and Research in International Relations, the influences of my past milieux were reflected in our simulation building: (1) My disposition was (and is) to want to order things with some rigor. (2) My predilection was (and is) to work in teams.

These proclivities influenced my work during the formation of the Inter-Nation Simulation. We built upon what others had delineated as the "actors" in international affairs—the decision-makers, their foreign offices, and the international organizations—all interrelated in an international complex. We might have gone on almost endlessly in the enumeration of variables characterizing these "actors." But if one were content with a limited number of variables drawn from each of the important domains, it seemed more likely that the researcher could get on with the construction. Certainly the political, economic, and military factors were prime, if one were building on what others had indicated. It was my habit to build by first specifying the entities with which I would work, then by characterizing these entities in terms of their attributes through the development of variables, and finally, in attempting to build "islands of theory" by interrelating some of these variables with others. [13].

With reluctance I omitted in this first approximation such aspects as "culture." In the attempt to link variables to one another, it was difficult to find solid work on which to build, given the state of theory about international relations in the mid-fifties [44]. Thus, relations among variables were sketched in a most abbreviated fashion in the Inter-Nation Simulation, omitting important "chunks," such as the interrelations between regional and universal international organizations. It was my pattern to tolerate gaps in my work, especially when the going became rough.

In my past research as I strove for adequacy as an experimenter, I had been accustomed to moving freely back and forth from field to laboratory and from laboratory to field. At Michigan, Donald G. Marquis, Roger W. Heyns, and I [28] had gone from the laboratory study of face-to-face discussion groups to observation in the field of on-going conference groups embedded in organizations making life-affecting decisions (see "A Bibliography from Conference Research," pp. 240-41 in [7]). At Carnegie Tech we had examined organizational hypotheses in our Controller's Study, both on the natural site and within our laboratory [38] and [21]. Thus, it now was important to attempt to construct a laboratory within which international phenomena might be studied, so that again both field and laboratory work might contribute to theory development. In addition, a simulation which might be operated with many replications seemed a useful tool for managing experimental intervention, so as to permit one to study consequences of new factors.

It was imperative to work with teams, inasmuch as the development and operation of the Inter-Nation Simulation was a task beyond my personal competence, given my knowledge, energy, and time constraints. Throughout the coming decade my proclivity toward working with others led to the formation of a variety of face-to-face groups. These included a "super-team" in the form of the International Relations Program itself at Northwestern, "sub-teams" through which I executed the Inter-Nation Simulation, and "side-teams" which served to stimulate and challenge my efforts as others went in alternative directions.

In the first year or two, decisions were made with respect to the Inter-Nation Simulation's (a) format and (b) contents. These decisions held with some firmness throughout the decade.

Simulation Format

In many ways the decision to use a mixed simulation involving both men and programs was easy. Yet this decision proved to be a significant one, in that it allowed a degree of rigor which is not present in the relatively unprogrammed political-economic-military exercise [2]. Further, it avoided the problems of the limits of our capabilities in attempting an all-computer construction, both financial and with regard to the state of the computer arts [12]. As a social-psychologist, I wanted to avoid attempts by the participants at role-playing which seems to be endemic to the political-economic-military exercise. How could the usual participant in the laboratory exercise—the high school senior or the college sophomore— imagine himself to be a decision-maker of another nationality operating within the international scene? As an organization theorist, I wanted to provide a set of constraints upon decision-making which were somewhat stable and objective, therein contrasting with the use of "umpires" whose human judgments about an on-going situation are fed into wargames in an ad hoc way. Having our decision-makers constrained by consequences derived from programs as well as from the reactions of component parts in other nations in the international system, it seemed possible to have a laboratory which may avoid these difficulties by incorporating both men and machines into a simulation format. By using quasi-abstract nations, the decision-makers occupy roles which are induced by the on-going situation and do not need to "play-act" strange nationalities. By using preordained programs there is no need for human "umpires" constituting a control team.

This decision with respect to the mix between men and programs coincided with another decision: the "nation" aspects of the simulation were to be programmed in the main, while the "inter-nation" aspects were to be left more or less free. Given the state of international theory in the late fifties, there was little more that one might do, inasmuch as what was called "international relations" was largely speculation about foreign policy-making [44]. Then, once the nations were operating as entities, the evolution of their interaction might be relatively unconstrained by programmatic features of the model. In this way it was hoped that the simulation construction might be of heuristic value, producing phenomena of an international character which would suggest new solutions to some of the problems extant in international affairs. Further, this delineation of "programmed" versus "free" aspects of the simulation coincided with well-agreed-upon notions that the internal features of a nation-state, such as "national interest," were important determinants of its external behavior, and vice versa—although fewer scholars subscribe to the point of view that the external environment of the nation importantly influences its domestic processes.

My multi-disciplined perspectives as an experimental social-psychologist and organizational theorist were satisfied through a man-machine simulation which allowed humans to operate within a constrained decision environment. The state of the computer arts in the late fifties precluded an all encompassing construction which my pragmatic commitment dictated; one then settled for a man-computer mix, for at least such a simulation was somewhat broader than the manual exercise focusing upon crisis. Given the fact that our knowledge of domestic affairs was more firmly grounded than our knowledge of international affairs, the social scientist could build eclectic programs for the nation with more adequacy than for the international system. As matters look in retrospect, these conditions of milieux provided the reasons why the Inter-Nation Simulation was constructed in the format of a man-program simulation.

Simulation Contents

In developing the contents of our simulation I joined in an ad hoc team with Robert Noel and Denis Sullivan in a set of pilot runs in which political, economic, and military aspects of the simulation were meshed together on the basis of intuition. By working within the three domains, we hoped to avoid a construction which would be "politics" dominated. In order to get the construction working, expediency was the order of the day. However, I do not think that we ever permitted our "theoretical objectives to be swamped by practical necessities" (see [17], p. 183 n.l). When we ran into a dead end, we attempted at times to circumvent the difficulty through omission, as we did in our troubles in developing an international public opinion component [33]. At other times we rationalized our way out of them, as in our decision that we would have no geographical component [15] inasmuch as our simulation was abstract and strategic in nature, with the consequences of geography being implicit in such devices as the comparative advantages of trade and in differential damage rates with respect to military operations.

Sullivan was immersed in the textbook literature of international relations, disentangling relationships which might be included in our simulation [4]. Noel with his background of economics was preparing for a more thorough treatment of some features of our construction [32]. My role was largely one of effecting integrations and serving as an inhibitor for much which might otherwise have been incorporated, so that the simulation would remain workable. By conducting pilot runs, we constantly checked whether the simulation bogged down when it was in operation, either because it was beyond the managerial capabilities of a staff or impossible to learn within reasonable time limits by the participants. A detailed chronology of three of these runs is presented by Noel elsewhere [33].

Members of the "super-team"—the International Relations Program at Northwestern—provided a milieu from which it

was difficult to escape. Colleague Chadwick Alger continual-
ly reminded us of the importance of international organizations, so that our simulation would not be a simple interstate
system. In the end, we but loosely incorporated an international organization as part of the Inter-Nation Simulation (see
[15], pp. 145-47). Colleague Snyder barraged us with variables to be included, as we attempted to winnow the many
candidates for inclusion as programmed variables. For example, we aborted the early attempt to implement motivational
directives, as delineated in the 1954 monograph by Snyder,
Henry W. Bruck, and Burton Sapin ([45], pp. 137-71, especially pp. 153-54); our posited "national goals" tended to limit
the operation of the situational factors (see [33], p. 73). On
the other hand, it proved feasible by physically separating the
participants to avoid some "small groups" effects, representing instead a quasi-bureaucratic structure in "Communication and Information" processes, as outlined by Snyder,
Bruck, and Sapin ([45], pp. 124-37). In the end, we sought
to placate our critics as to whether or not we had included the
variables in which they had especial interest by designating
"prototype" variables which were supposedly representative
of a gamut of political measures or economic processes or military capabilities (see [17], p. 253; [15], pp. 105-6). In this
way we were able to keep the entire construction within
bounds. The use of prototypes served to increase the level of
abstractness of our model (see [17], p. 253). This orientation
meshed with our attempt to posture the entities as typical
nations—large and small, developed and developing, aggres-
sive and co-operative (see [15], pp. 138-39)—so that, as our
decision-makers took their positions within these components
of the simulation, they might avoid "role-playing," reacting
instead directly to the imposed realities of their national situations.

Throughout the development of our simulation we presented our definitions of the variables used and our equations programming their inter-relationships to ad hoc groups within our International Relations Program. It was a salutary experience to defend one's choices—even though in the case of the relationships among the variables we operated largely without empirical foundations. Throughout the work our skills in verbal analysis were tested; at times, we found mathematics a useful complementary tool in developing our formulations, as has been explained in some detail elsewhere (see [16], cf. pp. 25-28 for discussion of variable development; cf. pp. 31-36 for discussion of use of equations).

At the time it seemed the factor analyses of Cattell were not adequately established to be utilized as an important guide in our variable selection. Yet, such a procedure would have enabled us to have cut through the plethora of variables, choosing those which were more unitary in conception. However, we were again stimulated to want improvement with respect to this part of our work, whence came the spin-off of the Dimensionality of Nations project at a later date, in collaboration with a "side-team" consisting of Rudolph Rummel and Jack Sawyer [36]. In retrospect it is provocative to report that we had accepted Hans Morgenthau's popular theory with respect to the national security function (see [17], p. 256). but had rejected Cattell's work. Yet the former exhibited no more empirical substantiation in the work of Lewis F. Richardson [35] than had been obtained by the factor analyses of the latter [5]. Do these decisions indicate we were willing to give more weight to the eminence of a sage than to the weight of his empirical evidence, as we brought our intuitions to bear in selecting variables and formulating the relationships among them? Perhaps it might have been wiser to have also used Cattell's factors as variables, rather than the intuitively constructed "prototypes" actually employed in the formulation of the Inter-Nation Simulation.

Before proceeding to an examination of the nature of the model itself considered from a meta-theoretical point of view, let me recapitulate. The working "sub-team" which constructed the simulation, along with the "side-teams" and the "super-team" of the International Relations Program in which this "sub-team" was enmeshed, provided rich substantive milieux. The variables and relationships used in composing the man-machine simulation of the international system, known as the Inter-Nation Simulation, were selected within these milieux largely in terms of intuition, as sharpened by the socio-intellectual pressure of our peers. A vague sensing of a ceiling to the complexity which would be practicable played an important role in forcing consolidation and omission of various features of the simulation, especially as the limits of feasibility were checked-out in pilot runs. As Noel has indicated, the evolution of the simulation certainly was of a "prescientific character" (see [33], p. 101-2).

Now consider what had occurred from a metatheoretical viewpoint. It became increasingly clear, as we went from pilot run to pilot run in 1957 through 1959, that our participants were not serving as human subjects within an experimental situation, as it had been my custom to regard those who took part in the experiments at Michigan and Carnegie Tech. This laboratory situation was different, in that our human participants were acting as surrogates rather than as experimental subjects in their own right. In the development of our national entities it was our intention to use abstract representations, so that all participants, regardless of nationality, could man any of the nations and act in terms of the simulated environment within which they would find themselves. Likewise, in our formulations of variables through the use of prototypes, a more abstract simulation was being developed. In fact, had the work in simulated thinking been further along [39], it might have seemed useful then to have employed all-computor components as decision-makers within our Inter-Nation Simulation. Instead, it was practical to use human beings as "black box" surrogates. Thus, our simulation was not really a laboratory counterpart of field behaviors. As it gradually developed, the Inter-Nation Simulation was rather a theoretical construction complemented by the verbal and mathematical formulations.

Awareness of this state of affairs was perhaps the most important "decision" which happened to us in the decade in which I have lived with the Inter-Nation Simulation. It is an orientation far from that accepted by many. Although admitting their own work is theoretical, some all-computer simulation people often are unwilling to accept the notion that humans and groups can serve as components within an operating model, despite my attempt to ease their discomfort by calling such "black boxes," in the jargon of the systems engineers. And, on the other side, my colleagues in social-psychology sometimes insist that I am simply operating noisy, poorly controlled experiments in which too many variables are being permitted to move simultaneously in providing a simulated environment for our subjects.

The Operating Model

Inasmuch as the Inter-Nation Simulation is a man-program model, involving humans as surrogate decision-makers and manually-computed or machine-computer programs in intimate interface, along with a structure of materials in ordinary language (through couriered messages and mass communication media), work with the model consists in its realizations, so that the initial starting conditions plus its contents are operated to yield consequences or outputs. Once the pilot work was done, it was feasible to utilize the simulation as an operating model in a somewhat systematic way. The bulk of our energy has been devoted to its utilization in the exploration of a large variety of phenomena within international affairs.

Simulations differ centrally from other theory constructions in the fact that they operate from initial conditions, unfolding consequences which their builders have not been able to explicate through verbal or mathematical manipulations. Once the pilot work has been completed, utilization of the simulation in quasi-experimental ways [4] is of critical import. In retrospect, employment of the Inter-Nation Simulation seems somewhat orderly; in actuality, its evolution has been a conjunction of researchers and contents happening to be available at the moment. Even though it is now possible to indicate that in our use of the simulation an attempt was made to explore its value in the replication of a past, in the duplication of a present, and in the projections of a future, our choice of experimental problems was somewhat fortuitous.

Had it not been for Richard Brody's concern with the proliferation of nuclear capabilities, it is doubtful that this attempt to understand the "Nth-Country Problem" would have been first on our experimental agenda. It is fortunate, also, that Michael Driver, then at Princeton University, was willing to collaborate in the work, so that multi-leveled characteristics could be studied. Driver [9] worked on the problem of the impact of personality, finding those with a complex cognitive style use force less often than those with a simple, more concrete orientation. Brody [3] was concerned with systemic processes, finding that when nuclear capability spreads, alliances tend to fragment. This "sub-team" worked with remarkable autonomy, as I stood by rationalizing their research.

The exploration of the crisis during the summer of 1914 leading to World War I was undertaken by the Hermanns because of the availability of support for summer work from Project Michelson, as well as because of the existence of a corpus of data which could be used in tailoring the simulation to fit the historical situation [25], [48].

Once again a multi-level approach could be used, inasmuch as Margaret Hermann was able to work with the personality materials, while Charles Hermann worked at a more systemic level with the political contents of the crisis [23]. In this work our attempt to disguise the situation in abstraction for our participants failed; it turned out that about half of our decision-makers recognized that we were simulating the pre-events of World War I. Through the mentoring of colleague James Robinson of our International Relations Program, the Hermann team soon became a "side-team" as they mounted a frontal attack upon such crisis behaviors through the Inter-Nation Simulation format after making considerable revision of its contents [22] and [24]. Their work exhibits the importance of a multifactor approach, in that crisis behaviors were induced, in the main, only when there was a perceived concomitant occurrence of their three components of crisis: an (1) unanticipated (2) endangering of important national interests with (3) pressure for immediate decision.

The increasing importance given by my peers to validity considerations in experimental work stimulated further work in the comparison of the Inter-Nation Simulation with empirical materials obtained from political, economic, and military studies of international affairs—the reference system. Recognition of the need for validation combined with our interest in doing something in a contemporary way. When the "sub-team" of Dorothy Meier and Arthur Stickgold undertook a series of runs moving forward from 1964 to a year or two into the future, the design of a past-present-future exploration across time was achieved. Because our decision-makers are surrogates for actors in the international scene, it seemed appropriate, also, to check the compatibility of high school as opposed to college participants, and each against professional participants. With rare skill and a precious willingness on the part of Quaker Harold Snyder of the Washington Seminar to aid in our recruitment, Meier and Stickgold were able to operate the simulation with foreign diplomats from the international community in Washington serving as decision-makers, as well as with our customary participants—high school and college students.

As we proceeded with these realizations representing past, present, and future situations, the same simulation model was being used by others throughout the United States and in a few places in Europe and Asia. In our Northwestern "shop" modifications of the model were constantly being made, although none seemed to be of major scope, therein constituting a series of "step-changes." All these seemed to derive from the same sources used in composing the original formulation—from intuitive assessments of incongruities (as in Meier's and Stickgold's [31] use of a budgeting process in order to dampen fluctuations in the allocations made of Basic Capabilities) or through attempted matching of the simulation with empirical findings (as in adjustment of parameters to approximate conditions during the summer of 1914 by the Hermanns [23]). As findings poured in from other researchers, it was possible to make a summary assessment of the extent to which the simulation model was describing the world reference system it was designed to represent. On the basis of some twenty-three studies, Guetzkow [18] noted that approximately one-third of the fifty-five comparisons between simulation and reference materials made within these researches revealed "Much" correspondence, another one-third revealed "Some," while in thirteen instances the simulations failed to produce (or produced but weakly) the phenomena of the "real world." Only four times did a simulation model produce an outcome which was an opposite or an inversion of a finding from the international reference system.

Thus, in our experimental realizations of the Inter-Nation Simulation in operation, we were guided by attempts to match empirical data, either existing or to be created, all at a level which was not too concrete, so that applications of our research would not be restricted to particulars.

Concluding Remarks

On the eve of the decision to construct a simulation, the state of our knowledge in the last half of the fifties provided constraints. Working habits and intellectual styles proved throughout the decade to be important determiners of how the construction of a man-program simulation of the international system would be implemented, both in its pilot stages as well as in its experimental phases. The particularities seem rather fortuitous: the "objective" social scientist being buffeted by the interests of research personnel, by the availability of research materials for construction of contents, and by the strong influences of peers and other research teams in the environment.

It is gratifying to note that in providing grand opportunities for the building of the simulation model in all its variations, the milieu provided by our sponsors—the foundations and the U. S. government—was salutary, helping to insure that our work was focused and productive, as we from time to time presented reports of past work and justifications for future activity to these monitors. Yet building a model of such a grand—almost preposterous—design has had repercussions on the builder. In the process of developing within the intellectual milieu of a multi-disciplined approach, I became a "marginal" scholar, little understood by many members of the very disciplines which served as seed beds. My attempt to embody the substance and methods of the behavioral sciences in the development of a simulation model of international affairs has led me into constructions which seem suspect and alien to some in today's policy community. Ten years of life with the Inter-Nation Simulation have been most demanding, I confess. After experiencing the pangs involved in confronting the problems of peace and war through the use of a simulation which is perhaps "too big" and "too soon", a number of my younger colleagues became disillusioned and have fallen by the wayside. Seeing our travail, most of my older colleagues have kept their distance—perhaps with wisdom.

The call for a retrospective essay came at an appropriate time, inasmuch as in the very academic year of our symposium on "The Process of Model-Building in the Behavioral Sciences" at the Ohio State University, an associate from overseas, Paul Smoker, has constructed and operated a new simulation model, the "International Processes Simulation" [43], representing a compromise between an incremental and a step-change. Building upon many of the products of our collaborators, including Richard Chadwick [6], Charles Elder [10], Robert Pendley [34], John MacRae [26], and Dina A. Zinnes [47] as well as on his own work [41] and [42], Smoker has developed a greatly enriched simulation model. But even now, Smoker has found it necessary to continue working in the man-program format, although the operation has been complemented by an on-line, time-shared computer for rapid feedback to the decision-makers participating in the simulation. Without the decade of work that was done on the Inter-Nation Simulation, this move to the International Processes Simulation would have been impossible.

At the present time there seem to be two central barriers to the rapid building of more satisfactory simulation models of the international system. It is imperative to have computer-aided instruction facilities available for mounting the realization of man-program simulations. A PLATO-like [1] or System Development Corporation–like [30] set of interconnected consoles for the decision-makers, interlaced to a central computer, is necessary to insure a less "noisy" operation. Such an arrangement would permit more adequate instruction of the participants as they learn the intricacies of their offices, would forestall mechanical errors in the course of the operation of a run, and it would permit rapid analyses of the outputs upon completion of each realization [20]. Secondly, it is imperative to generate a "bank" of componential computer programs, so that various researchers need not start from scratch, as radical reorientations are developed in the formulations of other simulations ([19], pp. 15-21). Yet, the development of such programs in turn depends upon two states of the art—the use of all-computer simulation in the social sciences generally [14] and the consolidation of an empirical base in reference materials in the international system [40]. Just as in the past decade in the development of the Inter-Nation Simulation we were importantly dependent upon our social and intellectual milieux, so in the decade ahead—when, I anticipate, forward strides will completely dwarf past efforts—we once again will be influenced mightily by those milieux, as we build the next generation of simulation models about peace and war.

Literature Cited

1. Bitzer, D. L., Lyman, E. R., and Easley, J. A. "The Uses of Plato: A Computer Controlled Teaching System." *Audiovisual Instruction,* 2 (1966), 16-21.

2. Bloomfield, L. P., and Whaley, B. "The Political Military Exercise: A Progress Report." *Orbis*, 8 (1965), 854-70.

3. Brody, R. A. "Some Systemic Effects of the Spread of Nuclear-Weapons Technnology: A Study through Simulation of a Multi-nuclear Future." *Journal of Conflict Resolution*, 7 (1963), 663-753.

4. Campbell, D. T. and Stanley, J. C. "Experimental and Quasi-experimental Designs for Research on Teaching." In *Handbook of Research on Teaching*, ed. N. L. Gage. Chicago: Rand McNally & Co., 1962.

5. Cattell, R. B., Bruel, H., and Hartman, H. P. "An Attempt at a More Refined Definition of the Cultural Dimensions of Snytality in Modern Nations." *American Sociological Review*, 17 (1951), 408-21.

6. Chadwick, R. W. "Developments in a Partial Theory of International Behavior: A Test and Extension of the Inter-Nation Simulation Theory." (Ph.D. Diss., Northwestern University, 1966).

7. Collins, B. E., and Guetzkow, H. *A Social Psychology of Group Processes for Decision-Making.* New York: John Wiley and Sons, 1964.

8. Deutsch, K. W. et al. *Political Community and the North Atlantic Area: International Organization in the Light of Historical Experience.* Princeton, N. J.: Princeton University Press, 1957.

9. Driver, M. J. "A Structure Analysis of Aggression, Stress, and Personality in an Inter-Nation Simulation." (Institute for Research in the Behavioral, Economic, and Management Sciences, Institute Paper No. 97). Lafayette, Ind.: Herman C. Krannert Graduate School of Industrial Administration, Purdue University, 1965.

10. Elder, C. D., and Pendley, R. E. "An Analysis of Consumption Standards and Validation Satisfactions in the Inter-Nation Simulation in Terms of Contemporary Economic Theory and Data." Evanston, Ill.: Department of Political Science, Northwestern University, 1966.

11. Goldsen, J. M. *The Political Exercise: An Assessment of the Fourth Round.* Santa Monica, Calif.: RAND Corp., D-3640-RC, 1956.

12. Gorden, M. "Burdens for the Designer of a Computer Simulation of International Relations: The Case of TEMPER." In Davis B. Bobrow and Judah L. Schwartz, eds., *Computers and the Policy-Making Community: Applications to International Relations.* Englewood Cliffs, N. J.: Prentice-Hall, Inc., 1968. Pp. 222-45.

13. Guetzkow, H. "Long Range Research in International Relations." *The American Perspective*, 4 (1950), 421-40.

14. ———, ed. *Simulation in Social Science: Readings.* Englewood Cliffs, N. J.: Prentice-Hall, 1962. Pp. 82-94.

15. ———. "Structured Programs and Their Relation to Free Activity within the Inter-Nation Simulation." In Harold Guetzkow, Chadwick F. Alger, Richard A. Brody, Robert C. Noel, and Richard C. Snyder. *Simulation in International Relations: Developments for Research and Teaching.* Englewood Cliffs, N. J.: Prentice-Hall, 1963, Pp. 103-49.

16. ———. "Some Uses of Mathematics in Simulations of International Rela-

tions." In John M. Claunch, ed., *Mathematical Applications in Political Science*, Dallas, Texas: Arnold Foundation, Southern Methodist University, 1965. Pp. 21-40.

17. ———. "Simulation in International Relations." *Proceedings of the IBM Scientific Computing Symposium on Simulation Models and Gaming.* York, Pa.: Maple Press, 1966. Pp. 249-78.

18. ———. "Some Correspondences between Simulations and 'Realities' in International Relations." In Morton A. Kaplan, ed. *New Approaches to International Relations*, New York: St. Martin's Press, 1968. Pp. 202-69.

19. ———. "Simulations in the Consolidation and Utilization of Knowledge about International Relations." In Dean G. Pruitt and Richard C. Snyder, eds., *Theory and Research on the Causes of War.* Englewood Cliffs, N. J.: Prentice-Hall, 1969. Pp. 284-300.

20. ———, Bitzer, D. L., and Hicks, B. "A General Strategy in the Incremental Development of IPS through PLATO." Dittoed. Evanston, Ill.: Simulated international processes project, Northwestern University, 1965.

21. ———, and Simon, H. A. "The Impact of Certain Communication Nets upon Organization and Performance in Task-Oriented Groups." *Management Science*, 1 (1955), 233-50.

22. Hermann, C. F. "Crises in Foreign-policy Making: A Simulation of International Politics" (Ph.D. diss., Northwestern University, 1965).

23. Hermann, C. F., and Hermann, M. G. "Attempt to Simulate the Outbreak of World War I." *American Political Science Review*, 61 (1967), 400-16.

24. Hermann, Margaret G. "Stress, Self-Esteem, and Defensiveness in an Inter-Nation Simulation" (Ph.D. diss., Northwestern University, 1965).

25. Koch, H. E. with the staff of the Stanford Studies in Conflict and Integration. "Documentary Chronology of Events Preceding the Outbreak of the First World War: 28 June–6 August, 1914." Mimeographed. Stanford, Calif.: Stanford University, 1959.

26. MacRae, J., and Smoker, P. "A Vietnam Simulation: A Report on the Canadian/English Joint Project." *Journal of Peace Research*, 4 (1967), 1-25.

27. March, J. G., Simon, H. A., and Guetzkow, H. *Organizations.* New York: John A. Wiley and Sons, 1958.

28. Marquis, D. G., Guetzkow, H., and Heyns, R. W. "A Social Psychological Study of the Decision-Making Conference." In Harold Guetzkow, ed., *Groups, Leadership and Men*, Pittsburgh, Pa.: Carnegie Press, 1951. Pp. 55-67.

29. McClelland, C. A. "Applications of General System Theory in International Relations." *Main Currents in Modern Thought*, 12 (1955), 27-34.

30. Meeker, R. J., Shure, G. H., and Moore, W. H. "Real-Time Computer Studies of Bargaining Behavior: The Effects of Threat upon Bargaining." *AFIPS Conference Proceedings of the 1964 Spring Joint Computer Conference*, vol. 25. Baltimore, Md.: Spartan Press, 1964. Pp. 115-23.

31.   Meier, Dorothy L., and Stickgold, A. "Progress Report: Analysis Procedures, Event Simulation Project—INS 16." Xeroxed. St. Louis, Mo.: Social Science Institute, Washington University, 1965.

32.   Noel, R. C. "A Simplified Political Economic System Simulation" (Ph.D. diss., Northwestern University, 1963).

33.   ——. "Evolution of the Inter-Nation Simulation." In Harold Guetzkow, Chadwick F. Alger, Richard A. Brody, Robert C. Noel, and Richard C. Snyder, *Simulation in International Relations: Development for Research and Teaching.* Englewood Cliffs, N. J.: Prentice-Hall, 1963. Pp. 69-102.

34.   Pendley, R. E., and Elder, C. D. "An Analysis of Office-Holding in the Inter-Nation Simulation in Terms of Contemporary Political Theory and Data on the Stability of Regimes and Governments." Mimeographed, Evanston, Ill.: Department of Political Science, Northwestern University, November, 1966.

35.   Richardson, L. F. *Arms and Insecurity: A Mathematical Study of the Causes and Origins of War,* ed. Nicholas Rashevsky and Ernesto Trucco. London: Stevens & Sons, 1960. Pittsburgh, Pa.: Boxwood Press, 1960.

36.   Rummel, R. J., and Diem, W. J. *Dimensions of Nations.* Forthcoming.

37.   Schramm, W., ed. *The Process and Effects of Mass Communication.* Urbana, Ill.: University of Illinois, 1955.

38.   Simon, H. A., Guetzkow, H., Kozimetsky, G., and Tyndall, G. *Centralization vs. Decentralization in Organizing the Controller's Department.* New York: Controllership Foundation, 1954.

39.   Simon, H. A., and Newell, A. "Computer Simulation of Human Thinking." *Science,* 134 (1961), 2011-17.

40.   Singer, J. David, ed. *Quantitative International Politics: Insights and Evidence in World Politics. International Yearbook of Political Behavior Research.* Vol. 6. New York: Free Press, 1967.

41.   Smoker, P. "Trade, Defense, and the Richardson Theory of Arms Races: A Seven Nation Study." *Journal of Peace Research,* 2 (1965), 161-76.

42.   ——. "Nation State Escalation and International Integration." *Journal of Peace Research,* 4 (1967), 61-75.

43.   ——. "International Processes Simulation: A Man-Computer Model." Mimeographed. Evanston, Ill.: Simulated international processes project, Northwestern University, 1968.

44.   Snyder, R. C. "Toward Greater Order in the Study of International Politics." *World Politics,* 7 (1955), 461-78.

45.   Snyder, R. C., Bruck, H. W., and Sapin, B. *Foreign Policy Decision-Making: An Approach to the Study of International Politics.* New York: Free Press of Glencoe, 1962. Pp. 14-185.

46.   Sullivan, D. G. "Towards an Inventory of Major Propositions Contained in Contemporary Textbooks in International Relations" (Ph.D. Diss., Northwestern University, 1963).

47. Zinnes, D. A. "A Comparison of Hostile Behavior of Decision-makers in Simulate and Historical Data." *World Politics,* 18 (1966), 474-502.

48. ――――, North, R. C., and Koch, H. E., "Capability, Threat, and the Outbreak of War." In James N. Rosenau, ed., *International Politics and Foreign Policy: A Reader in Research and Theory,* New York: Free Press of Glencoe, 1961. Pp. 469-82.

Making Artists out of Pedants

This is not a proper scholarly paper. It is a report on an attempt to develop creative model building skills and enthusiasms in a group of students; on the analysis that led to the approach used; and on some impressions of possible problems and results. For the most part, and without apology, it is a report of a love affair—an infatuation with a problem, a group of lively students, a houseful of tolerant colleagues, and a half-dozen precocious models.

The problem is that of increasing analytical and model-building skills in the study of human behavior. The students are a group of undergraduates, predominantly freshmen, looking for some clues to the character of modern social and behavioral science; meeting a requirement for graduation; or filling in an hour between biology and the history of arts. Smart, often skeptical, and detached. The colleagues are a group of professors in anthropology, economics, geography, political science, psychology, and sociology. Committed to the development of a new breed of social scientist, they undertook to teach a course for which none were trained and to attempt to communicate a style normally reserved for the elderly years of postgraduate study. The models are a set of simple forms used routinely by students of individual and social behavior. Models of choice, of exchange, of adaptation, of diffusion, and of structure; the foundations of analytical social science.

To a certain extent the love affair is with a specific course ("Introduction to Analysis") at a specific institution (University of California, Irvine). But much more basically it is a plea for a serious revision in the basic strategy for teaching introductory behavioral and social science.

Diagnosis

I consider it a self-evident proposition that an increase in the amount of creative model building carried on within the social and behavioral sciences would be desirable. Patently, the proposition is not self-evident except by proclamation. The point to the proclamation is simply to avoid the necessity of arguing the case and to turn directly to the question of means.

We wish to modify our program so that the next generation of scholars will be radically less incompetent than we are. We can accomplish this objective through some mix of two basic strategies:

1.   We can change our style of teaching and the content of what we teach.

2.   We can change the raw material (i.e., the kind of students) that we teach.

These are not independent strategies; generally one reinforces (or interferes with) the other. A change in curriculum, teaching style, or course content changes the decisions of students with respect to interests. A change in the kind of students creates pressure for us to make our program consistent with student interests and capabilities. The distinction between the strategies is important because we tend to view the problem of teaching as being associated primarily with the first strategy—what we teach to whatever students appear before us. It is my impression that we should attend much more consciously and systematically to the problem of the second strategy—the raw material that sits before us. Consequently, I turn first to an examination of the question of who sits before us.

Let us assume that recruitment into the social and behavioral sciences is not some random process but produces some systematic biases in the motivations, attitudes, and abilities of social science students. Students make choices that at least in some modest way match their expectations about a field with their own aspirations and their own view of their personal abilities. Counseling from parents, friends, and teachers guides a student into a commitment to a set of attitudes and experiences that are relatively consistent with his talents. As a result, students with greater interest and aptitude in art are disproportionately represented among art majors, and students with greater interest and aptitude in mathematics are disproportionately represented among mathematics majors. In a reasonably efficient "market" these simple mechanisms serve to allocate students to interests and careers in a way that is sensible even though it may deviate somewhat from the purity of a perfect market and explicit calculations of comparative advantage.

Consider the following overly simple model of the process:

1.   There exists a set of alternative fields (e.g., political science, history, mathematics).

2.   Initially a child has no preferences among these fields; he develops preferences on the basis of experience, tending to prefer those in which he is successful; he modifies his subsequent experiences (insofar as possible) to increase his experience in fields that are preferred.

3.   There is a set of basic ability dimensions (e.g., verbal fluency, problem-solving, imagery). Success in the various

fields depends upon the possession of some combination of these talents; the talents leading to success in the various fields are not identical but overlap considerably.

4.   Each child is characterized by a value on each basic ability dimension. Although the correlation among these values is strongly positive, it is not perfect.

Such a model is hardly adequate to explain all features of the choice of major; it does, however, capture (or at least is consistent with) the major features of currently received doctrine (a) about individual abilities, (b) about the relation between talent and performance in a field, and (c) about individual learning of preferences.

Within this model, the process by which preferences are developed is simple. The child is presented with a series of opportunities to choose an academic interest; he makes a choice on the basis of his preferences; he experiences some level of success or failure that depends on the relation between his abilities and the abilities necessary for success in the field; he modifies his preferences among the various alternative interests on the basis of his success.

It is clear that this process will tend to match up abilities and interests, that the speed of commitment to a field will depend on the variance of abilities in the individual (i.e., those whose abilities are relatively specialized will become committed earlier than those whose ability levels are relatively equal for a wide range of fields); on the relative specialization of the field (i.e., fields requiring abilities that are not required by other fields will tend to secure commitment relatively early); and on the general level of ability of the individual (i.e., those with relatively high ability will tend to become committed before those with relatively low ability).

According to this model, the social and behavioral sciences would tend to recruit those students with high abilities in relevant areas, although it would lose some "high social science ability" students to other fields when those students also had high abilities relevant to the other fields (thus particularly to fields with heavy overlap in the abilities required for success). Subject to "errors" in allocation due to chance elements in rewards and time limitations on experience, the process allocates students to the places in which their abilities lie.

Before considering the implications of this model somewhat more carefully, it may be well to note two conspicuous factors that have been ignored by this gradual commitment model of the way in which students select a field of interest. (1) The outside press of "market" value. A strict adaptation model ignores anticipations of future economic and social successes associated with various occupations and thus with various fields. At least some of the enthusiasm for medicine as a career stems from expectations on the part of students (and their parents) of the economic and social position that such a career confers. (2) The outside press of social norms. The appropriateness of certain fields (and certain talents) for certain people is regulated by social rules as well as by adaptation of intrinsic talent. Most conspicuous among such rules are the regulations related to ethnic group status and sex. It is relatively easy to secure agreement within the culture on the relative "masculinity" of various fields and of various talents; and the variation in values attached to fields by different ethnic groups forms the basis for a part of our ethnic folklore (e.g., "Knighthood is no job for a boy who is Jewish!").

This description of an individual adaptation model subject to the outside press of the market and social norms is reasonable. It is also *prima facie* neutral. But if it is correct—and I believe it basically is—the behavioral and social sciences suffer from three major disabilities.

First, virtually nothing of the behavioral and social sciences is taught in the first twelve years of school. The exceptions are insignificant and unfortunate: geography (i.e., maps, place

names, and the distribution of natural and human resources),
civics (i.e., constitutional and legal forms), and modern history comprise the normal fare (perhaps supplemented with
an exposure to sex and family living). In some schools there
is an effort to introduce a token bit of economics, psychology,
cultural anthropology, or sociology, but they touch an insignificant number of students late in their pre-collegiate days.
"Social studies" in the American school is frequently history
with an hour's discussion of current events on Friday.

Second, the skills required in the social and behavioral sciences are far from unique to those sciences. If we assume that
the skills required for a modern social or behavioral scientist
are the skills of analysis, model-building, hypothesis-forming,
data-interpreting, and problem-solving, it is clear that we
deal in widely demanded skills. In particular, it seems obvious
that such skills are highly correlated with (or identical to)
the skills involved in mathematics and natural sciences.

Third, the social norm press toward social science tends to
be antianalytical. The behavioral sciences are associated
(quite appropriately) with human beings and social problems. As a result, they are associated (quite inappropriately)
with a rejection of things, quantities, abstractions. They tend
(except for economics and political science) to be relatively
"feminine."

When we superimpose these facts on the basic model, we
obtain a series of disturbing predictions:

1. Since the abilities appropriate to high performance in
the social and behavioral sciences are similar to, or correlated
with, the abilities appropriate to success in fields commonly
offered at the precollegiate level (e.g., mathematics, natural
science, history, English), most students with high potential
for work in social science will have learned to prefer (and
have a strong commitment to) another field by the time they
come to college.

2. A disproportionate share of those students who say they

want to be social scientists on entering college will be "residual students," students who have not as yet found a field for commitment. In effect, this means they will be students who are not good at mathematics, physics, chemistry, English, history, biology, or foreign languages.

3.   Insofar as a student has learned to prefer social science in his precollegiate training, he will have learned to prefer social science in terms of some combination of current history–current events, social and human problems, and institutional description.

The fundamental problem can be stated in a grossly simple way: the students we have are either inept at the skills we need or persuaded those skills are irrelevant; the students with the skills we need are strongly committed to a competitive field long before we have access to them at college or graduate school.

If this description has validity, and if we wish to increase the model-building capabilities in the social and behavioral sciences, our objectives are clear. At all levels, we must:

1.   Recapture our "fair share" of the analytical abilities. For all practical purposes this means exposing the excitement of analytical social science to significant numbers of students already committed to the natural sciences, engineering, and mathematics. According to our model, we can recruit committed physicists if we can provide them with success experience in social science paired with lack of success in physics. Further according to the model, persons committed to physics are likely to have a comparative strength in analysis, they are likely to be more successful in a relatively "hard" behavioral science course than in a relatively "soft" one. Since a diminution of success in physics is assumed for some, we wish to create a setting for them to engage in model-oriented be-

havioral science, at every level in the academic hierarchy. This means (in most college settings) providing courses that take model building seriously but do not require previous exposure to the behavioral sciences—for freshmen, for upper classmen, and for graduate students.

2. Convert the interest and commitment in the behavioral sciences stemming from the outside press of market or social norms into a commitment to the artistry of model building. Those students who choose the behavioral or social sciences because of social norms (e.g., "females should help people") or because of occupational preferences (e.g., "I want to be a lawyer") are less prone to the perverse ability selection process outlined earlier. They are likely to be misguided with respect to the nature of the field, but they may have substantial latent analytical talent. It must be developed and rewarded early so that the nature of the game is redefined. This means (in most college settings) an early, intense exposure to the critical, analytical tricks of the trade.

3. Discourage an interest in social science on the part of those with weak analytical ability or interest. A relatively large number of students expressing an initial interest in social or behavioral science have a misguided idea of the nature of the field. Left uncorrected, this idea leads them to bad career choices, to a corruption of other student perceptions, and to a pressure on the faculty to adapt to the misreading. Here again, the requirement is for an early exposure to modern behavioral science.

A Program for a First Course

Any reasonable interpretation of the diagnosis above focuses considerable attention on the first collegiate course in the behavioral sciences. Whatever else we do is conditioned by the attitudes and styles developed in that course. For many students the first course will be the last. For almost all students it is the first authoritative communication they receive on the nature of the social and behavioral sciences. If some skill and enthusiasm for model building is not provided here, we incur heavy costs in the kind of students we attract and repel, in the styles students adopt, and in the mutual expectations of students and faculty. As a result, we delay serious training in the analytical tools of the trade until graduate school (or later).

Consider in this light the present character of the first exposure to behavioral science—the introductory course. Quite simply, with the possible exception of economics and despite major recent improvements (e.g., in sociology), most first courses in this domain portray the fields as a large collection of definitions loosely connected by important empirical generalizations.

Sociology I typically introduces a variety of new concept names (e.g., anomie, status, role). Each name is rather painstakingly defined and used to label some phenomenon. Some major phenomena of social behavior are discussed in terms of the new labels.

Geography I is typically a compendium of information on landforms, climate, vegetation, residential and industrial patterns, and the distribution of natural and human resources in the world.

Anthropology I ordinarily combines some relatively detailed descriptive exposure to exotic cultures with special category names for major institutions (e.g., kinship systems, life styles, and political organizations) and with a treatment of the evolutionary history of early man.

Psychology I typically defines a number of new terms (e.g., secondary reinforcement, authoritarianism, anticipatory gratification, cognition). In addition, the student is introduced to the major findings and illustrative research results.

Political Science I is most commonly a course in American government and politics. It catalogues the major legal and political facts of American public life, including the history and names of the major institutions.

Economics I ordinarily combines the rudiments of economic theory with varying amounts of descriptive material on the institutions of modern market systems and the problems of making them function in the United States.

These courses can be exciting and interesting for a student. The knowledge they contain can be useful, indeed indispensable to the professional social scientist. But the skills they provide have to be balanced against the message they communicate about the field.

As a group (but not equally) they emphasize three important intellective skills:

1. *Reading.* The courses typically impose substantial reading requirements. A student is expected to read, digest, and remember the material in a textbook of 700-900 pages plus several outside readings (e.g., "What are the differences between the Crow and Omaha kinship systems?")

2. *Organizing.* The student is expected to be able to discuss the material presented in terms of several different category schemes (e.g., "Compare and contrast political party structure at the national and local levels." Or "Show how the present structure of the Republican party has resulted from a few major developments in American political history.")

3. *Labeling.* The student is expected to be able to describe phenomena in the standard terminology of the field (e.g., "How does a child learn to imitate his father?")

The skills of reading, organizing, and labeling are fundamental skills. They are not, however, the major skills needed for imaginative theoretical social science. As a result, the usual first course in social science in the United States does two important things: (*a*) It develops secondary skills before primary skills, and thus places a false cast on later work; (*b*) It confuses students (and through them faculty) about the nature of the field. It encourages students with a comparative advantage in the wrong skills to continue in the program; it encourages others not to continue. As a result, substantial mismatches occur. In short, our present introductory courses do not face up to the problems posed by our diagnosis.

If reading, organizing, and labeling are the minor skills, what are the major ones? Major in this case is defined as those skills that should be taught at an early stage so as to form a lens through which subsequent training is focused and so as to recruit the "right" students into the field.

My list has no great uniqueness. It seems plausible and has the virtue of forming a basis for constructing an educational program. It is one man's list of those things with which every proper social scientist should feel comfortable:

1.   A basic ability to abstract from reality to a model. Problems in the social and behavioral sciences are *prima facie* enormously complex. They are frequently extraordinarily personal. It is necessary—but not easy—to form abstract simplified models of the conspicuously intricate reality. This simple talent is so obvious and so important that most of us disastrously forget a simple fact: the chances are nil that any of our students have *ever* approached social science problems in this way. Neither their precollegiate social studies training, nor their normal reading, nor their experiences at home or with peers prepares them for considering modes of analysis that require abstracting systematically from the real world.

2.   A facility at derivation within an abstract model. The

usual student in social science is totally inexperienced in deriving implications from a set of assumptions in a model. The kind of pre-mathematical reasoning involved in such activities is not mysterious, but it does profit from practice.

3. Competence in testing the derivations of a model through concrete empirical predictions. Here the critical problem is not to dwell upon the philosophic issues of "model" vs. "theory" vs. "prediction" but to provide actual experience in associating models with real data. In particular, we seek the experience of predicting successfully and (probably of greater importance) unsuccessfully.

4. A small collection of generally useful basic social science models. The number of models in social science is very large. But a few of them (e.g., a rational model of individual choice) are extremely pervasive and should be part of the repertoire of any new social or behavioral scientist. It seems important to insist not only that the student have a "modeling style" but also that he have command of a number of simple standard models and that he be skilled in applying this basic kit to a wide variety of situations.

I think I can summarize the major emphasis here quite simply: It is to develop the *artistry* of thinking analytically about social science. The focus on analysis as an art form is not empty. It is intended to communicate the importance of the aesthetic excitement, creative imagination, and unanticipated discovery to be found in creating models in social science. It is an art form that is learnable, indeed has a rather explicit technique. Practice leads to improvement. But for someone steeped in the pedantic tradition of social studies, any significant effort in this direction will come as a major surprise, indeed as a shock.

In identifying the necessary skills in this way, I explicitly reject two alternative approaches to the first course. First, we could construct an exposure to scientific methodology in general and social science metheodology in particular. This is a relatively familiar strategy and one with the logic of proper order behind it. Nevertheless, I think it is a mistake. It tends to substitute the erudition of method for the erudition of definition, a significant but not adequate improvement. It emphasizes the logic of criticism rather than the logic of invention.

A second rejected alternative is to emphasize the problems of social science, to permit the student to experience the excitement of real pressure for solutions stemming from the world around him. The tactic is to involve the student first in the reality of the world and from that to motivate a concern for dealing with it analytically. Such a tactic seems plausible to me. I reject it (with modest confidence) out of a feeling that in the context of the world in which we live creating a sense of social awareness among artists at problem-solving is rather easier than creating a sense of theoretical excitement among social observers.

Assuming that I have accurately defined the present situation and am correct in my analysis of the critical role of the "first course" (whenever it occurs), we can now turn to the concrete problem of creating such a course. The first course could be an upper division course without prerequisites, intended for non-behavioral scientists; it could be a similar course at the graduate level; it could be taught in the high school. I do not mean that the courses at those various levels would, or could, be the same; but I do believe that there are more first course situations than the freshman year. To establish concreteness, however, take as a reasonably familiar objective the problem of developing a one-year course to be taught to freshmen. This course should, against the background of the attitudes and expectations of students in social and behavioral science, accomplish three things:

1.   Develop the skills of analysis involved in taking a situation involving human behavior, abstracting from it to form a model, deriving the implications of the model, and identifying a set of empirical predictions.

2.   Provide a set of simple models of general utility in the social and behavioral sciences.

3.   Communicate the pure enjoyment of artistry in models.

These may well be impossible objectives. Certainly, they are not done easily at the level of the first course. However, after two years of trying (along with my colleagues) to do it, I am convinced that it can be done and that we are on the right general path; I am convinced that some rather exciting things happen when you try. In the remainder of this section I want to describe the major strategies of one specific course and illustrate them with some materials. A set of course materials for light evening reading may be found in the Appendix.

We required decisions both on the substantive content and on the format of the course, and it is clear that both must deviate significantly from the usual pattern.

With respect to substance, our basic hueristic has been to select a set of models that are (a) widely used, (b) relatively simple, (c) easily modified to extend their scope, (d) suggestive of the varieties of kinds of mathematics that might apply to models in the behavioral sciences, but (e) do not immediately require more than high school mathematics.

We have considered six major areas:

1.   *Individual choice.* The processes by which individuals choose among alternatives, make decisions, and solve problems. For example, investment behavior, gambling, voting, occupational choice, consumer behavior, the selection of mates. The basic model used is a model of rational choice

under risk. The student is introduced to the fundamentals of decision trees, of expected value calculations, and of alternative criteria for rational choice. The rational model is then applied to a variety of choice situations found throughout the study of human behavior.

2. *Collective choice.* The ways in which collectivities of individuals reach mutually satisfactory joint decisions. In particular, we consider such problems as choice within committees, groups, organizations, and societies. The basic model used is a power model. The student is exposed to a simple force version of power models found in sociology, political science, and psychology and then exposed to applications in such areas as the family, communities, international affairs, and organizations.

3. *Exchange.* Exchange as a special case of individual and collective choice. The student is introduced to the basic ideas of indifference curves and to the ways in which mutually acceptable trades are made in the market, the cold war, small groups, marriage, and politics. A good deal of emphasis is placed on being able to apply the basic model, drawn largely from economics, to a variety of "non-economic" situations.

4. *Adaptation.* Modification of behavior by individuals and collectivities in response to experience. The basic model is a weighted average of experience model as represented, for example, in common models of perceptual learning and in stochastic learning models. The ideas are applied to learning, personality development, socialization, organizational change, attitude change, and cultural change.

5. *Diffusion.* The spread of behaviors, attitudes, knowledge, and information through a society. The basic models are borrowed from epidemiology and include both simulations of contact, transmission, and contagion and simple versions of

differential equation models of the spread of a "disease" over time. The models are applied to the spread of fads, innovations, rumors, political allegiances, emotions, and ideas with special attention to the effects of social structure on the pattern and rate of diffusion.

6. *Structure.* Models for structural regularities in groups, societies, beliefs, attitudes, cognitions, and interpersonal relations. The basic model is a simple structural balance model elaborated into a more general discussion of rules for structural consistency—the "clumping" of things. The model is applied to attitude structures, kinship structures, language structures, group structures, and cognitive structures.

These six varieties of models comprise the basic substantive structure of the course. By the end of the year a student should be able to apply any of these basic models to any reasonably well-defined social or behavioral situation for which it is relevant. He should be able to take almost any situation of interest to a social scientist and make a somewhat reasonable first approach to asking theoretically meaningful questions about it.

With respect to format there were two basic decisions: First, we essentially eliminated text material as a central form for the course. Second, we substituted a focus on a weekly set of problems.

The reduction in text material is dramatic. During a quarter in which a freshman might read 1000 pages in history and 1000 pages in English literature, he has a few "suggested readings" of background articles. In part, the decision on reading was dictated by the content; we had no available text. But it was also a deliberate attempt to break away from reading as the primary mode of study. We wished to dramatize and enforce a rejection of the classic pedantic style.

In effect, we assume a Gresham's Law of Study: Reading

drives out thinking. The "law" is obviously overstated; reading can be an important creative activity; our hunch, however, was that it ordinarily was not. Rather, we suspected that the concept of "studying" denoted to many students the idea of obtaining information from a source, organizing it, and learning appropriate labels for the organized material. Moreover, we strongly suspected that a choice between "reading" and "thinking" would be resolved in favor of "reading"—primarily because it is a well-defined technology at which students are comparatively competent, provides information on progress and completion, and can be accomplished with certainty in some easily predicted time period. We sought to force attention on the main thrust of the endeavor by eliminating the excuse of an overly attractive secondary one.

In making such a unilateral decision to reduce reading to a minimum, we clearly incurred one possible major cost. If Gresham's Law of Study is correct, it should apply across courses. If the student is overloaded with reading already, reducing the reading load in one course simply reduces the proportion of time the student devotes to that course. Simultaneously it produces two feelings according to some students: (1) a feeling that the course demands little from him; (2) a feeling that he has no sense of how to "study" for the course if he is doing poorly. Such costs clearly were incurred. In balance, I suspect—but cannot demonstrate—that the reduced time had no adverse effect on the learning.

The second major decision was to focus the course on a series of problems. "Problems" here refers to something more analogous to an exercise than to a "social problem." Each problem was designed to require a student to exhibit some model, explore its implications, use it as a basis for policy, or discuss its empirical validity. Every week students are required to prepare answers to a series of problems. The problems are scaled from simple "cookbook" exercises to rather complicated social questions. In effect, the problem replaces the text as a form for student work. Lectures and discussions highlighting the kinds of models being used simply supplement a basic commitment to the problems.

Consider, for example, the following typical problem in diffusion.

Suppose that divorce in a society spreads in the following way:

i. Any couple in which both sets of parents were never divorced is very unlikely (probability $= 0$) to seek a divorce.

ii. Any couple in which one set of parents was divorced is somewhat more likely (probability $= p$) to seek a divorce.

iii. Any couple in which both sets of parents were divorced is much more likely (probability $= 1$) to seek a divorce.

A. If you assume that interest in marriage and marital choice are independent of parental divorce, that never-divorced parents have (on the average) the same number of children that divorced parents do, and that "initially" (i.e., about 1860) approximately 5% of all first marriages ended in divorce, what will be the rate and pattern of divorce in this society over time?

B. What differences would you expect in A if you assumed that children of divorced parents were more likely to marry other children of divorced parents?

C. What differences would you expect in B if you assumed that the more children a couple has, the less likely they are to seek a divorce?

D. If these models were correct and we wished to inhibit divorce in the society, what social action should we take? Show what difference it would make.

E. Comment on the validity of the models, using data wherever possible. If you suggest modifications, discuss the implications of the modifications.

In this case, the student is provided with a quite explicit model and asked to work through some of the implications. The use of divorce as a behavior that diffuses is a deliberate suggestion of the possibility of using diffusion models in cases that do not appear to be directly analogous to rumor transmission.

Or consider the following example from a problem on exchange.

Most males and females in the United States pair off in monogamous marriages. This pairing is sometimes fruitfully viewed as a "marriage market."

A. Specify a model of the marriage market. What "goods" are exchanged? What affects the distribution of those "goods" in society? What are the problems facing a rational participant in the market?

B. From your model, derive a series of predictions about marriage. For example, what will be the relative ages of husband and wife? Who (i.e., people with what attributes) will marry young? Etc.

C. Indicate how you would test your predictions and insofar as possible do so.

D. Discuss the limitations of your model. What assumptions are most dubious? What makes them dubious? What other kinds of problems are there?

Here the model is left somewhat less explicit but with some broad hints.

Finally, consider a typical short problem designed to clarify special features of analysis.

Suppose a man has the choice of living in either of two countries:

Country A: If he says "beer," he receives Coors or Olympia with equal probability; if he says "coffee," he receives Maxwell House or Yuban with equal probability.

Country B: If he says "Mo," he receives Maxwell House or Olympia with equal probability; if he says "Cy," he receives Coors or Yuban with equal probability.

Assuming the man is rational, which country would he prefer? What are the implications for a theory of natural languages?

None of these problems are particularly profound—though each, despite its simplicity, has some reasonable relation to the situation involved. Each leads to some valid predictions.

The main thrust, however, is not that; the main thrust is to expose a student through a course of more than 100 such problems to the pleasures of simple model building in social science.

Epilogue

At the outset I indicated that, for the most part, this is a report on a love affair. It will come as no surprise, therefore, to discover that I think the experiment is a success. But it may be useful to comment on the major observable (or semi-observable) outcomes. I think there are five basic comments:

First, *the approach is controversial*. It is controversial among students. It is controversial among the faculty in behavioral and social science. It is controversial among our colleagues in other fields. The variance in attitudes appears to be considerably larger than it is with most courses. The attitudes seem to be somewhat more violently held.

Second, *it can be done*. Although the experience has been in some ways quite harrowing, we have been able to live with our basic decisions. We have been able to generate the materials required, to provide sufficient continuity in meaning and contents to make for most students a meaningful experience most of the time.

Third, *it works*. It works in the sense that many students—and some quite spectacularly—become facile and interested in the model building game. Each of us has his favorite illustration of this phenomenon. Mine concerns the case of a classroom discussion of the following problem:

> Suppose that Mary each week divides her limited "boy friend time" between Harry and John so as to maximize their joint value to her. Now suppose that John is drafted and that Mary must restrict the time "with" John to letter writing (which takes some fixed amount of time less than she previously spent with him). Is it possible that both of the following empirical generalizations could be true?
>
> 1. Out-of-sight, out-of-mind.
> 2. Absence makes the heart grow fonder.

The main issue, of course, involves a discussion of shifts in the overall time allocation and in the marginal rate of substitution as a result of the change. But the high point of the discussion was not the illustration of the model and its implications. It was a young lady who raised her hand and said, "Do you realize that you have proven concave women are monogamous?"

The course also works in the sense of influencing student choices of major fields of interest. The course, in conjunction with a mathematics requirement, has apparently influenced substantially the propensity to choose a social or behavioral science as a major. Although it is not easy to establish with our available data the details of the shifts, both casual observation and some indirectly relevant data suggest that while the proportion of undergraduate students who are majoring in social science has remained essentially constant at Irvine, the composition of majors (in terms of interests and special talents) has probably shifted in the direction of greater analytical abilities.

Fourth, *it is hard to teach.* If the course were a kind of cafeteria of individual disciplines, it would be possible to organize it so that psychologists taught the psychology, economists the economics, etc. Since it attempts to mix the various disciplines substantially, and to emphasize a few general models, each faculty member is driven to teaching not only in a relatively unfamiliar style (i.e., the problem focus) but also in relatively unfamiliar domains. It has neither a textbook for students nor a "secret text" for faculty.

Fifth, *it is vulnerable.* It is vulnerable in part because it is successful. Since the explicit objectives are viewed by some as pernicious, success is viewed as dangerous. It is vulnerable in part because it violates student expectations. It is vulnerable in part because it is difficult to teach; it has not always been taught well; it cannot be taught casually.

One of the grander traditions of love affairs is that neither the commitment to them nor the pleasures to be gained from them depends on guarantees of permanence. We have, I believe, taken a useful step in the direction of creating a program that develops skills and enthusiasms for creative model building in a group of college freshmen. It is a first step. It is not a unique first step. It is not unreservedly successful. With impatience, intolerance, and imagination it can serve as a basis for making the first exposure to social and behavioral sciences relevant to the excitement of those disciplines and for providing to a fortunate few of us the exquisite delights of corrupting the young.

On the Art of Modeling[1]

The process by which the experienced management scientist arrives at a model of the phenomenon he is studying is probably best described as intuitive. The term "intuitive" refers here to thinking which the subject is unable or unwilling to verbalize. Indeed, really effective experienced persons in any field typically operate in a largely intuitive manner and view with impatience attempts to make their methods explicit. The experienced management scientist may well consider questions as to how he selected the variables to be included in the model, how he decided which were to be regarded as random, and so on, as so trivial that they cannot occupy his serious attention or so non-trivial that they cannot be answered. He is perhaps willing to regard the abstraction and translation of a management problem into a scientific problem as an art in the sense that it must remain largely intuitive. Any set of rules for obtaining models could have only the most limited usefulness at best, and at worst, might seriously impede the development of the required intuition.

If one grants that modeling is and, for greatest effectiveness, probably ought to be, an intuitive process for the experienced, then the interesting question becomes the pedagogical problem of how to develop this intuition [2]. What

---

1. Reprinted by permission from *Management Science*, August, 1967, Vol. 13, No. 12.

can be done for the inexperienced person who wishes to progress as quickly as he can toward a high level of intuitive effectiveness in management science? What can be done for the experienced person whose mind "draws a blank" when seeking to model some management problem? Can we say only, "Get more experience, for it is the chief source of intuitive development and the only recourse when intuition fails?" In what follows, an effort is made to verbalize about the process of developing models in a very limited fashion and to consider the role of such verbalizations in the educational process. In attempting to make the process of modeling explicit, it may be reasonable to suppose that one is raising hypotheses about the process and that one is providing a possible target for imitation when intuition is insufficiently developed. It does not appear reasonable, however, to suppose that one could provide a general "recipe" for making models, nor that one could do very much more than modestly enhance the process of developing intuition. It may well be that intuition or artistic skill is largely the product of imitation and practice, yet this process of development must have a beginning. Experience suggests that this beginning must include more than simply a familiarity with other people's models.

Justification and Discovery

A basic distinction that must be communicated to the inexperienced is the difference between the "context of justification" and the "context of discovery" [4]. Management science (and all science) is reported and communicated in the form of a logical reconstruction which aims at providing a justification for the inferences produced. This logical reconstruction has little if anything to do with the psychological process by which the inferences were first obtained. It is the custom in science to report a piece of work by stating the assumptions of premises which determine the model, showing the deductive steps by which the relevant consequences of the model were obtained, and then reporting the design and analysis of the experiment aimed at testing the hypotheses suggested by the consequences of the model. All this is very much *ad hoc*. The danger for the inexperienced is that, finding little else in the literature of their science other than such justification, they will begin to assume that this is a description of the process of discovery.

The experienced scientist knows that the psychological process is very different, but he seldom attempts to verbalize it. One may wonder, however, whether even those with considerable experience do not sometimes practice a little delusion of themselves and their colleagues by tending to read ad hoc justifications as descriptions of the context of discovery. One often senses that a writer is implicitly saying, "See how logical, how methodical, how brilliantly inevitable was our progress in this study." Since all of the writing in a science is likely to be of this sort, one must conclude that the experienced persons in a field are not of great help to the inexperienced, so far as the art of modeling is concerned. In fact, the inexperienced may be led far astray if they begin to imitate the logical process in seeking to develop their own intuitive skill. It is not at all clear that the teaching of models by exposing the inexperienced to the *ad hoc* contributes much to the development of creative model building ability. Indeed, this is the fundamental criticism that might be made of management science education. The teaching of modeling is not the same as the teaching of models. How then, is one to teach modeling?

Skill in modeling certainly involves a sensitive and selective perception of management situations. This, in turn, depends on the sort of conceptual structures one has available with which to bring some order out of the perceptual confusion. Models can play the role of giving structure to experience. Yet we seldom encounter a model which is already available in fully satisfactory form for a given management situation, and the need for creative development or modification is almost universally experienced in management science.

Three Basic Hypotheses

The approach to the development of model building skill which we have explored might be stated in the form of three basic hypotheses. It is of some importance to regard these statements as hypotheses, since no really systematic test of their effectiveness has been made.

1. The process of model development may be usefully viewed as a process of *enrichment* or *elaboration*. One begins with very simple models, quite distinct from reality, and attempts to move in evolutionary fashion toward more elaborate models which more nearly reflect the complexity of the actual management situation.

This seems harmless enough, yet it is of some importance to point it out explicitly to the inexperienced. The attempt to begin immediately with a rather rich model may become a serious source of frustration. Starting simply gets things moving and thus tends to relieve some of the tension. It does, however, require a certain amount of poise or "guts" to back off from a complicated problem and begin with a simple conceptual structure. It requires one to deliberately omit and distort certain aspects of the situation and to knowingly commit the sins of suppressing difficult considerations and suboptimizing.

2. *Analogy* or *association* with previously well developed logical structures plays an important role in the determination of the starting point of this process of elaboration or enrichment.

Clearly, one point of teaching models is to provide such well developed logical structures which can be utilized more or less directly as starting points. It must be emphasized, however, that they typically provide only the starting points. When one asks if a given management situation can be modeled in the framework of linear programming, or waiting line theory, or inventory theory, what is really being asked is whether one of these structures will give a head start in the evolutionary process of obtaining a useful model. Sometimes the search for analogy calls forth broad general structures such as differential equations or probability theory, sometimes more specific and highly developed structures like waiting line theory, and sometimes very specific models developed especially for another management problem. While analogies are central to management science, we are concerned here with what steps should be taken subsequent to the discovery of such an association or when none appears possible. This is perhaps another way of saying that management science is an emergent science and a long way from handbook engineering which uses "off the shelf" models.

3. The process of elaboration or enrichment involves at least two sorts of *looping* or *alternation procedures*.

a. The alternation between modification of the model and confrontation by the data. As each version of the model is tested, a new version is produced which leads in turn to a subsequent test.

b. The alternation between exploration of the deductive tractability of the model and the assumptions which characterize it. If a version of the model is tractable in the sense of permitting the attainment of the analyst's deductive objectives, he may seek further enrichment or complication of the assumptions. If the model is not tractable or cannot be "solved," he returns to purify and simplify his assumptions.

The importance of the first of these looping procedures is to make clear that the research need not be conceived as one grand test of a single model. Nor need one decide whether to develop the model first or "get the data" first. It is of considerable consequence in management science to note that a part of the data consists of the attitudes of the client, not only toward the management situation being studied, but toward the management scientist studying it. The role of looping here has been previously explored [3].

The second of these alternations is the central concern of this discussion. Indeed, facility in modeling means, to a large extent, the selection and modification of basic assumptions which characterize models. Here again a certain poise is required to work with a variety of assumptions, some of which are more nearly in agreement with the analyst's conception of the management problem, while others may be productive of models more tractable from the viewpoint of his deductive abilities. The task is to discover a set of assumptions which are both usefully descriptive of the problem and deductively tractable. Implicit in this sort of proposition is the refusal to resort to simulation until a serious attempt at analysis has been made.

Whatever the relevance of these hypotheses for particular scientists, it has been our impression that conveying to the inexperienced the notion that modeling is a process with some such looping dynamics is essential. In the following section, the illustration of this in a particular instance is suggested.

Some Specific Hypotheses

In the process of attempting to develop modeling ability in inexperienced persons for a number of years, several specific suggestions have emerged. We regard these as hypotheses in the sense that no claims can really be made as to their general effectiveness. In situations where persons are very inexperienced, these suggestions appear to be helpful. At least they are better than no explicit remarks whatsoever about procedure, since they do prevent the inexperienced from being completely at a loss as to how to respond to the challenge of developing a model.

In presenting these hypotheses in the context of an example, it is natural to choose an example which furnishes a good illustration of the ideas, but in doing so one once again introduces something of the flavor of an *ad hoc* reconstruction. Clearly, things will not always work out as in the example and thus the suggestions cannot be rigidly interpreted or applied.

Suppose one undertakes the problem of designing a transportation system which is to serve a network of terminals on a fixed schedule. The locations of the terminals are known and some data is available or could be obtained on the time pattern of demand for transportation among the terminals. We suppose also that the criterion for a good design involves some measure of service furnished in response to the demands, combined with some measure of the cost of obtaining and operating the equipment to be used in the system. Clearly, considerable effort may be involved in bringing the study to this point of definition, and there are well known difficulties with making operational the criterion for a good system design. We will, however, suppress these considerations in order to emphasize the model building aspects of the study. We suppose that it becomes clear to the designer that he may determine the schedule of arrivals and departures to be specified by the timetable and the number of vehicles to be available for running out the timetable. He may attempt to produce directly a model which will predict the level of service, investment, and operating costs for any choice of timetable and number of vehicles. He may search for analogies to this problem among the well developed logical structures with which he is familiar. Suppose, however, that this effort is unsuccessful, and that he seeks to factor the system design problem into simpler problems for which models may be more readily obtainable. This is our first suggestion or hypothesis.

FACTOR THE SYSTEM PROBLEM INTO SIMPLER PROBLEMS

In this example the analyst might decide to consider:

1. The schedule design problem: Given a fixed fleet of vehicles, what schedule of arrivals and departures will give the highest level of service and still be within the capabilities of the available fleet?

2. The fleet size problem: If a schedule of arrivals and departures is given, what is the minimum fleet size which can accomplish it? (We have already allowed the assumption of homogeneous vehicles to creep in.)

An ideal factoring of the system design problems would yield simpler problems which could be modeled and would subsequently permit easy combination into a system model. When factoring occurs, the result is several problems whose solutions are sub-optimal or approximate from the viewpoint of the system model. For the inexperienced, this deliberate setting aside of the ultimate design objectives is often a very difficult step. Having done it, however, one may attack the simpler problems—for example, the fleet size problem.

ESTABLISH A CLEAR STATEMENT OF THE DEDUCTIVE OBJECTIVES

An essential early step would appear to be the achievement of a clear (but still tentative) statement of the deductive objective of the model. Do we want the model to predict the consequences of various policies? Do we want it to suggest an optimal policy? In the fleet size problem, suppose we take the deductive objective to be simply the determination of the minimum fleet size which can accomplish a given schedule of arrivals and departures. Such a statement provides the criterion for determining the deductive viability or tractability of the model. Yet in establishing such an objective, one should keep open the possibility that it may prove unachievable, or that different objectives may suggest themselves as the model is developed. The final deductive objective may be foreseen in advance or it may emerge as a surprising result of the study of the model.

SEEK ANALOGIES

At this stage, as well as at any other stage in the process, one should seek opportunities to make analogies between the problem at hand and some previously well developed logical structure. These analogies will often occur as a sort of intuitive leap. Is the problem a linear programming problem, a queuing problem, or an inventory problem? Is it usefully similar to one which has been modeled by someone else? Note that the possibility of an analogy ought to be considered even before the problem is very well defined, since analogies may well suggest the way in which the problem might tentatively be made more specific. We will suppose that the fleet size problem does not yield immediately to this search for analogies and it becomes necessary to take further steps.

We do not wish to give the impression here that the process of discovering analogies is easy or well understood, but only to suggest that it may be helpful to be somewhat self-conscious about it.

CONSIDER A SPECIFIC NUMERICAL INSTANCE OF THE PROBLEM

This is a key step for the inexperienced person. The specification of a simple instance of the problem is often difficult for the beginner, since it represents a retreat (hopefully temporary) from the generality and complexity which he ultimately seeks. The purposes of the specific example are at least three:

1.   To lead the analyst to make statements about the assumptions which characterize the example. It is these assumptions which may be a useful starting point for achieving greater generality.

2.   If the numerical instance can be "solved" by inspection, then perhaps the process of solution can simply be generalized.

3.   The specific instance provides a workable starting point for establishing a symbolism and giving general expression to some of the obvious things which are noticed in the specific case.

Suppose for example, we consider a network consisting of

terminals numbered 1, 2, and 3, which is to be served according to a timetable specified below. The timetable is based on an eight hour clock and repeats every eight hours.

Departure times from terminal 1: 2, 5, 8
"   "   "   "   2: 1, 3, 7
"   "   "   "   3: 1, 4, 7

The routings are given as: 1 to 2, 2 to 3, 3 to 1, and the running times on these routes are 2 hours, 1 hour, and 2 hours, respectively. This permits the construction of the complete time-table:

TERMINAL 1		TERMINAL 2		TERMINAL 3	
Arrivals	Departures	Arrivals	Departures	Arrivals	Departures
1	2	2	1	2	1
3	5	4	3	4	4
6	8	7	7	8	7

At this point one might discover by "inspection" or by "trial and error" that this timetable can be run out with a minimum of four vehicles. By asking how such a result was obtained and then generalizing, one may find the key to a workable model for the problem. If this fails, however, the example provides a basis for making some explicit statements about the assumptions which it implies. For example, we seem to be assuming:

a.   That the schedule must be met. No deviations from the specified departure times are permitted.

b.   That the running times are inclusive in the sense that they include the times for a vehicle to load and unload.

c.   That the running times are invariant. The possibility of breakdowns or delays is suppressed.

d.   That the number of arrivals and departures at each terminal will be equal during each scheduling period.

Perhaps there are other assumptions as well, but these begin to define the sort of problem which has been established. If we fail to achieve the desired result with these assumptions, we can come back and modify or relax some of them for another try. In this sense, the assumptions that an analyst presents first in a journal article were probably actually discovered last—as he did the work. The task is to discover a set of assumptions which lead to a tractable model, and to do this typically requires a number of attempts.

ESTABLISH SOME SYMBOLS

Perhaps the next step might be to translate the numerical example into symbolic terms. For some reason this is often a difficult step. One wants to choose symbols which are suggestive of their interpretations, and to give careful definitions of each. The beginner often fails here, and carelessness at this point has serious consequences later on.

Suppose for example, we elect the rather conventional double subscript notation. Let:

$a_{ij} = $ the time of the ith arrival at terminal j
$d_{ij} = $ the time of the ith departure from terminal j.

Now we are at a crucial point. What to do next? We suggest that in the absence of any useful insight, one simply writes down in symbolic terms some of the obvious things which can be seen in the numerical example. Our hypothesis is that giving expression to the obvious will be highly suggestive in terms of further steps in the development of the model.

WRITE DOWN THE OBVIOUS

What we have in mind are such things as conservation laws, input-output relations, ideas expressed in the assumptions, or the consequences of trivially simple policies. In the fleet size example, we might simply try to express the basic conservation law which states that the vehicles provided will spend their time either in making runs between terminals or sitting idle while waiting to depart. If we have a fleet of k vehicles available each scheduling period, we provide an input of kT vehicle hours, where T is the length of the period. These vehicle-hours will be devoted to either idleness (let $I =$ total vehicle-hours of idleness) or running (let $R =$ the total vehicle-hours of running). Thus the conservation law is

$$kT = I + R.$$

Hopefully such a simple statement will be suggestive. Perhaps in this case we notice that R is fixed by the specification of the timetable, and that to minimize k one must minimize I. What can one do to influence the amount of idle time? Since idle time is generated when a vehicle waits at a terminal for its scheduled departure, it must be that the way in which arriving vehicles are assigned to departures will influence idle time. At terminal 1, we might make the following matching of arrivals and departures.

TERMINAL 1		
Vehicle arriving at	Departs at	Idle time
1	2	1
3	5	2
6	8	2

This matching generates a total of five vehicle hours of idle time.

Before proceeding, it is worthwhile noticing a very important property of this system. So long as departure times are met, nothing which is done at one terminal can influence the idle time at the other terminals. This means the system can be "cut" in the sense that we can minimize idle time terminal by terminal, rather than having to consider the entire system at once. In symbolic terms the idle time at terminal j, I_j, is independent of the idle time at terminal k, I_k, and the idle time for the system is given by

$$I = I_1 + I_2 + I_3.$$

The real objective of systems analysis is not simply to study larger and larger problems, but to find ways of "cutting" large problems into small ones, such that the solutions of the small ones can be combined in some easy way to yield solutions for the large ones.

Using the numerical example, one might try some other matchings of arrivals with departures. We notice that if at any time more departures have been scheduled than there have been arrivals, the excess departures will have to be made by vehicles kept over from the previous scheduling period. One can easily write out all of the possible matchings, and note that a matching which keeps no vehicles over from the previous period generates 5 vehicle-hours of idle time; one which keeps 1 vehicle over generates 13 vehicle-hours of idle time; one which keeps 2 over generates 21 vehicle-hours of idle time—and so on. Thus, keeping down idle time seems to be associated with keeping down the number of vehicles kept over from the previous period.

Now this same insight can be expressed symbolically.

$$I_j = \sum_i d_{ij} - \sum_i a_{ij} + A_j T.$$

Here A_j is the number of vehicles kept over from one scheduling period to the next at terminal j. At this point the problem is "solved" in the sense that the minimum fleet size will result when we have minimized the A_j. Further examination of the numerical example may suggest that the A_j will be minimized when arriving vehicles are assigned to departures on a first-in-first-out basis. (There may be other policies which are as good, but there are none better than FIFO.)

All that remains is to compute the minimum fleet size. We may again return to the numerical example to compute the running time generated by the schedule. Using our symbolism, we might express this computation as:

$$R = \sum_i \sum_j a_{ij} - \sum_i \sum_j d_{ij} + BT.$$

Here B is the number of vehicles that depart in one scheduling period and arrive in the next.

Now the symbolism and the expression we have established begin to yield some interesting deductive consequences. It turns out that

$$kT = I + R = \sum_j I_j + R$$
$$= \sum_j A_j T + BT$$

and thus

$$k = \sum_j A_j + B.$$

Thus we can suggest, "Find the minimum number of vehicles which must be kept over at each terminal using a FIFO assignment policy. Add to the sum of these minima the number of vehicles which are on route at the end of a scheduling period, and the result will be the minimum fleet size." This result was originally obtained by Bartlett [1].

If we had not been successful, perhaps the next step would have been to return to the numerical example or to the assumptions, looking for ways to simplify and try again. As it is, we might wish to go on toward enriching or complicating the model.

IF A TRACTABLE MODEL IS OBTAINED, ENRICH IT. OTHERWISE, SIMPLIFY

One might, in our example, wish to consider different types of vehicles, running times which are random variables, schedules which change from period to period, breakdown and maintenance time for the vehicles, and so on. Generally speaking, one may simplify by:

—making variables into constants
—eliminating variables
—using linear relations
—adding stronger assumptions and restrictions
—suppressing randomness

Enrichment may involve just the opposite sort of modification.

Other Sources of Modeling Skill

Sensitivity to certain other ideas appears also to be associated with the achievement of facility in modeling. For example, it is obvious that a feeling of being at ease with mathematics is important. One of the reasons that one studies advanced mathematics that will probably not be "useful," is to achieve a more comfortable and relaxed grasp of less advanced mathematics which is likely to be used. Some appreciation of the various purposes which models may serve is helpful. Illustrating the use of models to give quantitative predictions, to give qualitative predictions, as data collection plans, as research plans, as perceptual sensitizers, as devices for structuring knowledge, and so on, tends to broaden one's view of the sorts of models which are worth developing and the different directions their development might take.

Similarly, attempts to develop a consciousness of some of

the characteristics of models appears helpful. Beyond the rough description of a model as "simple" or "complex," one might usefully consider:

Relatedness. How many previously known theorems or results does the model bring to bear upon the problem?

Transparency. How obvious is the interpretation of the model? How immediate is its intuitive confirmation?

Robustness. How sensitive is the model to changes in the assumptions which characterize it?

Fertility. How rich is the variety of deductive consequences which the model produces?

Ease of Enrichment. What difficulties are presented by attempts to enrich and elaborate the model in various directions?

Conclusion

The test of such hypotheses as these is, of course, whether they appear to enhance model-building skills. In making such an investigation, it is important to present the model building challenge or opportunity outside of any context which prejudices the result in an obvious way. Problems which are presented at the end of an extended discussion of some particular logical structure do not present the same kind of challenge as problems encountered outside of any such context. Similarly, exercises which require one to substitute numbers in previously developed models may help to bring familiarity with the models but they do not help to develop model-creating ability. A much more useful introductory device is to present a simple model and ask for enrichments in specific directions.

The central points, however, are that the teaching of models is not equivalent to the teaching of modeling, and that there is a difference between the context of justification and the context of discovery. We have attempted to raise here the hypothesis that some explicit suggestions can enhance the process of developing the intuitive skill associated with model-building.

Literature Cited

1. Bartlett, T. E. "An Algorithm for the Minimum Units Required to Maintain a Fixed Schedule." Mimeographed. Lafayette, Ind.: Management Science Research Group, Purdue University, 1956.

2. Bruner, Jerome S. *The Process of Education*. New York: Random House, 1957. While this paper deals only with some crude attempts to meet the educational problem, there is considerable relevant literature. Some representative examples include:

    Arrow, K. J. "Mathematical Models in the Social Sciences." In *The Policy Sciences*, ed. Daniel Lerner and Harold Lasswell. Stanford, Calif.: Stanford University Press, 1951.

    Beveridge, W. I. B. *The Art of Scientific Investigation*. New York: Random House, 1957.

    Ghiselin, Brewster, ed. *The Creative Process*. Berkeley: University of California Press, 1952.

    Hadamard, Jacques. *The Psychology of Invention in the Mathematical Field*. Princeton, N. J.: Princeton University Press, 1945.

    Kemeney, John G. *A Philosopher Looks at Science*. Princeton N. J.: Van Nostrand & Co., 1959.

    Simon, Herbert A. "Some Strategic Considerations in the Construction of Social Science Models." In *Mathematical Thinking in the Social Sciences*, ed. Paul Lazarsfeld. Glencoe, Ill.: Free Press, 1954.

3. Morris, William T. *Management Science in Action*. Homewood, Ill.: Richard D. Irwin, 1963.

4. Reichenbach, Hans. *The Rise of Scientific Philosophy*. Berkeley: The University of California Press, 1959. P. 231.

Analysis of the System
To Be Modeled

I would like to start, not at: How can we make a model?, but
at the even more primitive question: Why make a model at
all? By getting a clear answer here we shall, I hope to show,
obtain a firm foundation for the further developments. I have
frequently been impressed recently with how easy it is to jump
too quickly to questions of this type, only to find later that the
whole elaborate attack has been directed against a basically
inappropriate target.

I would like then to start from the basic fact that every
model of a real system is in one sense second-rate. Nothing can
exceed, or even equal, the truth and accuracy of the real system itself. Every model is inferior, a distortion, a lie. Why
then do we bother with models?

Ultimately, I propose, we make models for their convenience. We make models of an aircraft wing and put it in a
wind-tunnel because taking a real wing into the air is far more
expensive and dangerous. We write equations on paper to represent the flows of traffic through new highways, because it is
cheaper than building many highways and then scrapping all
but one. And sometimes the avoided "inconvenience" is extreme, as when we trace out, in a model, what *would* happen
if the water level of the Great Lakes were raised fifty feet, or
if planets were attracted according to the inverse cube.

The superlative convenience and accuracy of Newton's way of representing the gravitational actions of planets by a few pencil marks on paper has sometimes led to the idea that Newton's model is in some way inherently superior to the actual system—that in this model he somehow extracted what was valuable, the rest being mere clutter. Here I want to adhere to the other point of view, that the truth is the *whole* system, not any extract from it. I would point out here that however vigorously Newton's equations of motion are defended as the extreme in truth, the astronomer must always reintroduce the discrepancies, such as (until Einstein's work) the rotation of the perihelion of Mercury, when he would make *real* predictions. Ultimately, the raw facts are final.

Taking, then, the practical usefulness of models as a basis, the process of using a model can be formulated in a manner highly congenial to modern mathematics [5]. We start with the assumption that the scientist is interested in some process that will, or may, occur in the real world—a planet goes from its present position to where it will be in a year's time; a pile of steel girders becomes a constructed bridge; the present traffic chaos in a certain city changes to a smooth flow. This change, call it C, can be represented by an arrow going from the one state S_1 to the consequent state, S_2.

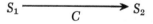

$$S_1 \xrightarrow{C} S_2$$

In the model there must be a corresponding change C' $\longrightarrow$, from one specification of planetary coordinates to another, or from one arrangement of lines on a drawing board to the final drawing of the bridge.

There must also be a rule of correspondence μ such that if we translate the real state S_1, using μ, into the model, there apply C', and then translate back, using the inverse μ^{-1}, we

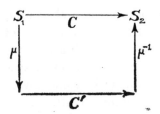

arrive again at S_2. Since the correspondence must (in a good model) hold for all pairs S_1, S_2:

$$\mu^{-1} C' \mu = C$$

(with a convention for the order of operation), in the sense that the single, direct operation C, in the real world, is equivalent to the triple operation $\mu^{-1} C' \mu$, going through the model.

The equality stated is necessary (if the model is to be a faithful one). It also makes clear the importance of the purely practical criterion that I have above called "convenience" (using the term very broadly). Use of the model demands three operations (μ, C', and μ^{-1}) instead of the single operation C. What science has found is that many cases exist in which the use of the three operations is actually more convenient than the use of one.

It seems to me that this purely pragmatic reason for using a model is fundamental, even if it is less pretentious than some of the more "philosophical" reasons. Take for instance, the idea that the good model has a "deeper" truth—to what does this idea lead us? No electronic model of a cat's brain can possibly be as true as that provided by the brain of another cat; yet of what *use* is the latter as a model? Its very closeness means that it also presents all the technical features that make the first so difficult. From here on, then, I shall take as a basis the thesis that the first virtue of a model is to be useful.

At this point I may refer to the possible objection that this formulation is not applicable to a system like the human brain, which may have some "random" or unpredictable aspects. To this I would reply that the scientist is essentially concerned with finding and using such laws as *are* present, the random aspects being usually relegated to such terminal classes as the residual error of an analysis of variance, or the probable error of an astronomical prediction. Again, when randomness is present in the actual events, as at Las Vegas, the *probabilities* may well be invariant and exact for a particular game, such as roulette; and the probabilities associated with a proposed new game may well be exactly predictable.

Thus the formulation given may well be appropriate to such aspects of the real system as have a law-obeying regularity. What I have to say will be relevant to those aspects.

The Multiplicity of Models

From this point of view, there is no such thing as *the* true model of such a complex system as a cat's brain. Consider, for instance, the following four possible models, each justifiable in its own context:

1. An exact anatomical model in wax.

2. A suitably shaped jelly that vibrates, when concussed, with just the same waves as occur in the real brain.

3. A biochemical soup that reacts biochemically just as does the cat's brain when drugs are added.

4. A programmed computer that gives just the same responses to auditory stimuli as does the living brain.

Clearly, complex systems are capable of providing a great variety of models, with no one able to claim absolute priority.

We are in danger, perhaps, of being led astray by the outstanding merits of certain well-known particular models. We rightly admire Newton's system of equations and laws and, after its great success, are apt to think that he discovered *the* model. I suggest that his model is widely used largely because pencils and paper are widely available, and *his* type of mathematics widely known. Had our circumstances been very different we might well have preferred a different model: had we lived, for instance, in a world where algebra was not a practicable process, but where many point-sources of light and many conical bodies made the geometric development of ellipses instantly available, we might well have found that wholly geometric methods were preferable to the algebraic.

With a multiplicity of models available, our real question becomes (assuming a model to be necessary): which one shall I choose? But before considering this question there is a highly relevant factor to be considered.

Bremermann's Limit

In my opinion, one of the most fundamental contributions to the epistemology of large and complex systems was made by Bremermann's demonstration [3,4] that there is a limit to the rate at which matter can transmit or process information. The limit rests on two of the most basic properties of matter (Einstein's Mass-Energy relation and the Uncertainty Principle of Heisenberg), so it is not likely to be overcome by any merely technical advance. Further, being so general it applies with equal strictness to the matter in a computer and to the matter in a scientist's brain. We are *all* subject to this limit.

Its actual value is 10^{47} bits per gram per second. This number may look large, but its importance comes from the fact that when we, as scientists, look at a complex system we may easily envisage processes that would require far more than this quantity. (Notice first that taking a ton of computer only adds 3 to the exponent; changing to nanoseconds adds only 9; and taking tons of computer and decades of time will not increase the number of bits processable beyond about 10^{70} bits.) Yet as soon as complex combinative processes are considered, the demand may go far beyond this limit.

As a simple example, suppose we have a square screen of lamps, with 20 a side, and thus 400 lamps in all. Let each lamp be only lit or unlit. The number of illuminated patterns that can be presented on it is 2^{400}, i.e., about 10^{120}. Suppose now that we ask some question about *grouping* these presentations, for instance: What grouping will best correspond with "looking like a cubist picture"? The number of dichotomies of 10^{120} objects is $2^{(10^{120})}$, so to ask for a particular dichotomy is to select one item from this last number of items. Until further information is available, this selection demands bits to the extent of its binary logarithm. Thus our apparently harmless question about the grouping of these pictures, on a basis of only a 20 x 20 screen, has latent in it a demand for the processing of 10^{120} bits—a quantity far beyond what is possible under the limit.

I need not give further examples, for it is very commonly found that as soon as we make an estimate, even the roughest, of how much information-processing is required when the system is complex and combinatorial, the estimate is beyond Bremermann's limit, often beyond to a degree far exceeding that shown by the example above. Far from being merely "theoretical," the limit is in fact outstanding as a practical obstruction.

It is on this basis that the method of "model-making" has an irrefutable claim as *better* than the study of the raw facts. The model, by replacing a system whose study would demand a transgression of Bremermann's limit, makes the study possible. From this point of view we transfer from system to model to *lose* information. When the quantity of information is small we usually try to conserve it; but when faced with the excessively large quantities so readily offered by complex systems, we have to learn how to be skillful in shedding it. Here, of course, model-makers are only following in the footsteps of the statisticians, who developed their techniques precisely to make comprehensible the vast quantities of information that might be provided by, say, a national census. "The object of statistical methods," said R. A. Fisher [8], "is the reduction of data."

Analysis

On this basis, the making of a model may find a firm justification (though making a model is not the only way of lessening the quantity of information).

Within the method of models there are various ways of proceeding. One of the ways that often helps to reduce excessive demands on the quantity of information-processing is that of "analyzing the whole into parts." Its mode of action depends on the following features.

When parts combine to form some whole, we often find that the quantity of information necessary to comprehend the whole increases, not proportionately to the number (n) of parts, but far faster, often exponentially, so that the quantity of information approximates to a^n, where a is some base. Now it is easily verified that when n and a are both large, the operation of dividing n by some quantity k and also multiplying the whole by k, resulting in $ka^{(n/k)}$, is to cause a very great *reduction* in the quantity.

"Dividing a whole into k parts" does just this. (Each is $1/k$th the size, so its complexity will approximate to $a^{(n/k)}$. But there are k parts, so the total quantity [if the interaction between the parts is negligible], becomes k times this.) When the interaction between the parts is not negligible, the fall is not as great, but it may still be worth while. When the parts are in *full* interaction with one another (every part having a direct and full effect on every other part) then there is commonly no gain at all. Then the method of proceeding by analysis is either futile or must be justified in some other way.

Thus, the method of analysis, sometimes presented as obligatory, is in fact a strategy for taking advantage of the situation (if it occurs) of the whole system's being composed of parts that do not have direct and full effects on one another. Thus it may well be a natural way to take advantage of such facts as:

1.   In a big city, not every person knows, or communicates directly with, every other person.

2.   In a brain, not every nerve cell is connected directly with every other nerve cell.

3.   In a big computer, not every part is directly affected by every other part.

To sum up, the method of analysis has no right to be regarded as the correct one, absolutely. It is, however, often a very powerful resource when one faces the obstruction of Bremermann's limit.

From now on, I shall assume that we are working within some specific problem for which it has been decided that the method of analysis is appropriate.

Finding the variables

The would-be model-maker is now in the extremely common situation of facing some incompletely defined "system,"

that he proposes to study through a study of "its variables."
Then comes the problem: Of the infinity of variables available
in this universe, which subset shall he take? What *methods*
can he use for selecting the correct subset?

To start at first principles, it may be taken as axiomatic that
the scientist, selecting a set of variables to be "his system,"
must either be arbitrary in his selection or must be guided by
reasons. The former case need not be discussed here, but the
case where he selects for reasons emphasizes that the selection
must be guided by some cause, or primary motive. Often there
is an obvious goal, but sometimes the worker, not having a
goal sufficiently specified, is plagued by uncertainty about
what to do towards selecting his variables.

It is here that a practical goal can be invaluable. In the behavioral sciences there are plenty: How reduce the delin-
quency in this town? How teach these students better? How
improve the viewing of this TV screen? Somewhere, then,
there must be a "generating question," able to provide a criterion for the various steps taken later. Without this primary
selecting factor, selection among variables can only be aim-
less and arbitrary. The primary question, therefore, is not:
What are my variables? but: What do I want? Under what
terms of reference am I working? Without a sufficiently practical knowledge of his criterion, the worker is indulging simply
in a random intellectual walk, in the hope that something interesting will turn up. As there is no *method* possible here, let
us restrict ourselves to the case when some sufficiently well
defined generating question exists.

The generating question will usually at once suggest a list
of variables; it is, however, merely provisional. The scientist's
next task is to bring the list to a condition of "completeness"
(to a degree sufficient for the main task). But before dis-
cussing the meaning of "completeness" we must make a point
clear.

The worker who has had some training in mathematics can only too easily fall into the habit (or trap) of thinking that a "variable" must mean a numerical scale with an additive metric. This assumption is quite unnecessarily restrictive, sometimes fatally so. The meteorologist has long worked with his five "types of cloud," the veterinarian with the various "parasites of the pig," the hematologist with the four basic types of "blood-groups." Modern mathematics, using the method of set theory, is quite able to handle such variables, which are often unavoidable in the behavioral sciences. What follows below will be written so as to be equally applicable to the metric and nonmetric variables (with obvious qualifications at certain points).

With a provisional list of variables the scientist's next task is to examine them in detail. In particular he will want to know of each: Is it relevant?

Tests for "relevance" have many technical forms though they all express the same basic idea. According to the type of investigation we may ask, of two variables X and Y:

1. Is the correlation (suitably defined) between X and Y zero?

2. Is $\delta X / \delta Y$ everywhere zero?

3. Is the transmission (in Shannon and Wiener's sense) between X and Y zero?

4. Are X and Y independent in probability?

5. If we changed Y, would X change?

All these forms (and there may be further variations) seem to be expressions of the basic idea in set theory: Is the relation between X and Y a *product* set?

It should be noticed that all these tests are ultimately operational: they can be brought to *demonstration*, and owe nothing to any argument of plausibility. It is worth noticing here that the test by demonstration is always treated as the ultimate test, let plausibility say what it will. Thus, on an after-noon in 1888, Heinrich Hertz showed two pieces of electrical apparatus with no trace of electrical connection between them. Yet after he had showed the correlation between their behaviors, sparks in the one following a switchclosing in the other, no scientist, whatever his philosophy, denied the valid-ity of the proof of *effective* connection. The operational test is the last court of appeal.

With this test (that some aspect of X's behavior is *condi-tional* on Y's value) available for all pairs of variables, the sci-entist's task is then logically simple. He looks for a set of vari-ables that (1) is clearly related to his primary generating question, and (2) is closed, or complete, in the sense that for every variable in the set, the variables that affect it are all already included in the set.

(Sometimes he will accept a weaker form, in which some of his variables are affected by other variables that are not in the set but are otherwise acceptable. These other variables are his "parameters." Only the generating question itself can de-cide what variables may be allowed this special relation to the set. In the theory of "machines," in the general sense, they are its "input.")

In this connexion it may be worth noticing that systems showing "memory" (specially common in the behavioral sci-ences) may, at least in principle, be treated by exactly the same method. All that is necessary is that some of the vari-ables in the set will be related to others by being the values of these others taken at some earlier time.

Before we leave the topic of "which variables," however, a word may be said on an aspect that must not be left unno-ticed: what if some of the variables are relevant only in com-bination, not individually? Here we open a topic of great difficulty and complexity, on which much remains to be said.

This richer possibility has already been encountered (in the history of science) in all the criteria of conditionality mentioned above:

1.   When the correlations between X, Y, and Z are all zero pair-wise, but some partial or third-order correlation shows that linkage is present.

2.   When the zero-ness of $\delta X/\delta Y$ depends on the value of Z, (which corresponds to examining the value of $\delta/\delta Z$ · $[\delta X/\delta Y]$, i.e. of $\delta^2 X/\delta Z\delta Y$).

3.   When $T(X:Y)$, the transmission between X and Y, is zero but the conditional transmission $T_Z(X:Y)$ is not.

4.   When X, Y, and Z are probabilistically independent, pair-wise, but not as a triple.

5.   When the effect of Y on X (e.g. a switch controlling a light) depends on the value of Z.

6.   When the ternary relation R is not a product set, yet all its Z-sections show a product-set relation between X and Y.

These examples show that we are now moving into the topic of the systems that show complex internal interactions. Here the complexities increase with extreme speed as we ascend to interactions of higher order. Bremermann's limit soon puts a stop to such explorations! The subject deserves extensive generalized study, for those who work in complex systems cannot afford not to be well armed with the right ideas. Fisher's general methods for the treatment of high-order interactions [9] are now well known, but they are not generally applicable, as there must be an outstanding variable on which a variance is meaningful.

A possible line of greater generality has recently been commenced [2], using the idea of "cylindrance," but the subject is still largely unexplored.

Beyond this point, so far as I know, it is impossible to go

while treating systems in general. Basically the worker is selecting (a set of variables from the multitude that the universe
offers). As a selector he is subject to the rule: Any system that
achieves appropriate selection (to a degree better than
chance) does so as a consequence of information received [1].
The necessary information may come from past knowledge
of the particular type of system, and also be won by trial and
error (with "experiment" as a specially efficient form of trial).

The process of finding a suitable set of variables may be
summarized:

1.   There must exist some "generating question" as primary
criterion. Without it, selection can only be arbitrary.

2.   The generating question must generate many possible
sets of variables. As the relation between question and set is
almost never one to one, there are often many sets that satisfy
the demand (in various ways and to various degrees): to
look for *the* set is often inappropriate. From these various sets
further selection can be made only by considering further details of the particular question.

3.   The work of selection ultimately becomes one of testing for independence between variables. The process is essentially the same whether it goes on through the statistician's
tests of significance, or through measures of the transmission
of information, or through direct experiments to test for
causes, or through the mental processes of the scientist, or
through the operations of a programmed computer.

Finding the Isomorph

Finding a suitable set of variables, however, is (as was said
earlier) only a means to an end. The end, in model-building,
is some relation (law, structure, pattern) isomorphic with the

relation in the real world. Sometimes the set of variables is almost obvious and the major part of the work is to find the relationship, the isomorphism. It is here that the myth of the "genius" may enter, to the exclusion of the scientific approach.

To the scientist, all selection is assumed to be subject to the postulate that appropriate selection (to a degree better than chance) is possible only on a basis of information received. He does not, in other words, admit the concept of "inspiration" as a factor in selection. How then, when he considers the model-making activities of (say) Newton or Gauss or Mozart is he to explain the known facts?

The answer may well be that a most valuable way of obtaining more information is by trials, and there is plenty of evidence that those who showed unusually high powers of selecting the right law, theorem, or chord did in fact do a great deal of work through trials, either on paper or in their heads. Newton, once asked how he solved so many problems, replied simply: "By always thinking about them." Gauss, iń a letter to Olbers [10], wrote:

Perhaps you remember . . . my complaints about a theorem which had defied all my attempts. . . . This lack has spoiled for me everything else that I found; and for four years a week has seldom passed when I would not have made one or another vain attempt. . . . But all brooding, all searching has been in vain. . . . Finally I succeeded several days ago.

Any idea that the genius goes straight to the solution clearly is inapplicable here, with its four years of "all brooding, all searching. . . ." The origin of this misconception may perhaps be revealed by the end of Gauss's letter [10], when he says:

. . . when I some day lecture on the topic, nobody will have any idea of the long squeeze in which it placed me.

Without intending any deception, Gauss may well have left some of the audience with the impression that he produced the method of solution instantaneously at the blackboard, and thus quite misled them into thinking that *his* processes (for choosing the appropriate method of solution) were not subject to the ordinary law of selection.

"Finding the isomorph" is, from this point of view, perfectly clear in its *general* principles. The isomorph may be deducible from available knowledge; but this process is not research, only an exercise in the application of the known. If present knowledge is insufficient for deduction of the isomorph, then more information must be obtained. There are many ways of obtaining more information—here I wish only to emphasize the importance of *trials* as a source, especially of those that occur, in a not specially orderly way, in the researcher's brain. Poincaré's well known description [13] tells how he made a discovery after taking an unusually large amount of strong coffee:

> A host of ideas kept surging in my head; I could almost feel them jostling one another, until two of them coalesced, so to speak, to form a stable combination.

My personal belief is that such "trials," whether semi-systematically as Gauss's, or quite randomly as Poincaré's, play a large part in every active research worker's progress. Speaking personally, for years my method of attack was to fill my thoughts freely at bedtime with the topic in hand, so that the problem could be seen in the clearest possible way—so that the utmost possible tension was created, in other words. "Sleep" followed, and I was often able, the next morning, to set the whole matter in a much clearer way. (Speaking psychiatrically, I can also say that the method has dangers and must be used with some knowledge of when to stop; but I do not think that intellectual success and psychiatric danger can be entirely dissociated.)

Such trials must be to some degree "at random," for the worker does not yet know where to try; but it is also clear that a Poincaré, or a Gauss, with a lifetime of experience behind him, will tend to conduct his trials in those ways on topics that offer, on the average, a better prospect for success than those chosen by a beginner.

The general rule for such selections may thus be stated: Use what you know to narrow the field; then, within it, make trials at random. Any rule that claims to be superior to this rule must necessarily involve some appeal to "inspiration," the action of some guiding factor not possessed by the worker.

The subject of "finding the isomorph," which includes some of the great triumphs of science, has been bedeviled by those cases where a guess turned out right, leaving us gasping at its unexpectedness. The subject will be seen in proper balance only when the historians of science are equally careful to record the outcomes of the other, less successful, guesses. William Hamilton, for instance, was certainly one of the outstanding mathematical physicists of the last century, and a maker of many discoveries; his method for treating complex dynamic systems, for instance, is still used by everybody today. He also developed a penetrating eight-dimensional algebraic method ("model") for understanding the nature of polarized light, at that time a great mystery. After several years' work he had his theory perfected, and the first experiment that it predicted showed it to be wrong. This is the *reality* of how the genius gets his results!

Extending the Model

In the behavioral sciences, any isomorph will have been obtained by comparison with facts from some portion of the real word, from some finite number of variables, and over a finite range of each.

Once the model has been made, the work of the model-maker has reached a temporary completeness, but usually he then immediately wishes to see whether the model's range of application may be extended.

The process of extension, if we are to stay within the framework of the ideas expressed in this paper, will be subject to just the same postulate as the other processes of selection; for, of all possible ways of extending, the model-maker naturally wants to select those that have some special property of relevance. Thus, a model of the brain in gelatin, that vibrates just like the brain under concussion, is hardly likely to be worth extension in the biochemical direction.

From this point of view the process of extension is essentially an exploration. So far as the worker does not *know* the validity of the extension, to that degree must he explore *without* guidance, i. e., "at random." Newton himself, after he had found the coherence of the astronomical facts, must have trembled when he first applied his model to earthly mechanics: however confident he may have been, he must have known that confidence can be misplaced.

A clear example of the uncertainties of extension occurred when Einstein, by expanding his relativistic formula for a moving body's mass, found it proportional to

$$m_0 c^2 + \tfrac{1}{2} m_0 v^2 + \ldots \text{ (negligible terms)}.$$

(where m_0 is its resting mass, v its velocity, and c the velocity of light). He noticed that $\tfrac{1}{2} m_0 v^2$ was the body's energy due to its movement, and wondered whether $m_0 c^2$ might correspond to some basic or "total" energy associated directly, in some unknown way, with its having mass m_0 [7]. Writing in 1920, Einstein admitted frankly that he had no idea whether it would prove to be significant, or to be just an algebraic artifact that must be ignored. Decades later it proved to be highly significant, showing that his original theory *was* extensible at that point, but here I wish to emphasize his admitted inability even in 1920 to say whether this extension would or would not sustain the isomorphism: only further explorations could tell. Ultimately, all arguments about plausibility must give way to further tests against the raw facts.

Models in the Future

A word on this topic may be of interest and may be specially important today if, as I believe, "model-making" in the future is likely to differ somewhat from that of the past.

The distinction lies essentially in the facilities available to the model-maker. Until about 1940, every model-maker had little more than the resources of pencil and paper, and of perhaps sixteen hours in the day. Every model that he made was subject to these restrictions and to the fact that his brain, as a material dynamic system, could not get through more than a certain quantity of information-processing in one life-time, with Bremermann's limit as the ne plus ultra.

Sometimes, as Newton found, a comparatively simple model can be isomorphic with an extremely broad range of phenomena; then we speak of his discovering a great "law," (not universal, however, for his "law" fails at the cosmic and nucleonic extremes). When this happens, the event is so striking and worthwhile that whole generations of later scientists take as their aim the finding of another such isomorphism.

I do not for a moment wish to suggest that no more such laws remain to be found, but it is true that most scientists cannot expect to be as lucky: much of their work, especially in the behavioral sciences, will have to be on the construction of isomorphisms that are not only of narrower range but are also much more complex in their structure.

Before 1940, models of really complex structure were both unconstructible, because of the labor involved, and unusable for the same reason, large quantities of information-processing being impossible. Today, however, much greater quantities of information can be processed, and we must expect the construction of "theories" (or models) of much greater complexity. Such models have already been built of such complex systems as the respiratory and cardio-vascular [11], the thermo-regulatory [12], and that of electrolyte distribution in living tissues [6].

I see no reason (in the really distant future) why all model-making, and in this I include all "law-discovering," should not be carried on, as a routine matter, inside computers. The basic processes of search must go on equivalently whether the mechanism is made mostly of copper in a factory-built computer, or mostly of protein in a living brain. In a sense, the problem of finding an isomorphism is trivial, for it has the logically irrefutable solution: generate all possible forms and examine them seriatim. If the set of forms has no structure, no constraint over it, *this solution cannot be improved on*, and computer and genius alike are reduced to simple drudgery. (As example: find a rule, as complex as is necessary, for relating the peoples' names, in the New York Telephone Directory, to their numbers. Unless the company uses some systematic method that imposes a constraint or "structure" on the relation, the "rule" will end by being as bulky, and complex, as the directory.)

Often, however, human questions have human answers, and here the experience imposed on us in a billion years of evolution and a few decades of personal learning may well find us humans able to select much more economically in questions of human types. (Similarly the digital computer can select much more economically when the structure is in any way related to the scale of 2.) When questions having a large "human" component occur, the human information-processor has a great advantage. But with this special advantage set aside, the processes that must be carried through when information is to be used in the making of models, finding laws, and finding constraints (all equivalent to recoding the information into a more compact form) can be performed alike by all law-abiding mechanisms.

My expectation is that behavioral scientists will have only one model of the human brain (with parameters to allow for age and similar factors). It will be essentially a large general purpose computer, kept at an international center. Initially it will have no specific structure, but more and more will be programmed into it as facts, physiological and psychological, become available. Gradually its behavior will become more and more recognizably brainlike. It will be a total archive of the time's knowledge, and it will, on demand, give (by doing) a prediction of the consequences implied by that time's knowledge. When the predictions are falsified by new experimental facts, the machine's structure will be altered. This is the way, as I see it, that we shall move from "Newton's theory of gravitation" to (300 years later) "the world's theory of the brain."

Literature Cited

1. Ashby, W. R. "Computers and Decision-Making." *New Scientist*, 7 (1960).

2. ———. "Constraint Analysis of Many-Dimensional Relations." *Progress in Biocybernetics*, ed. N. Wiener and J. P. Schadé. Amsterdam: Elsevier Publishing Co., 1965. Vol. 2, pp. 10-18.

3. Bremermann, H. J. "Optimization through Evolution and Recombination." *Self-Organizing Systems, 1962*, ed. M. C. Yovits, G. T. Jacobi, and G. D. Goldstein, Washington, D. C.: Spartan Books, 1962. Pp. 93-106.

4. ———. "Quantum Noise and Information." *Proceedings of the Fifth Berkeley Symposium on Mathematical Statistics and Probability*, ed. Lucien M. LeCam and Jerzy Neyman. 4 vols. Berkeley and Los Angeles: University of California Press, 1967. Vol. 4, pp. 15-20.

5. Coombs, C. H., Raiffa, H., and Thrall, R. M. "Some Views on Mathematical Models and Measurements Theory." *Psychological Review*, 61 (1954), 132-44.

6. DeLand, E. C., and Bradham, G. B. "Fluid Balance and Electrolyte Distribution in the Human Body." *Proceedings of IBM Scientific Computing Symposium on Simulation Models and Gaming.* New York: IBM, 1966. Pp. 177-93.

7. Einstein, A. *Relativity: The Special and General Theory*, trans. Robert W. Lawson. New York: Henry Holt & Co., 1920.

8. Fisher, R. A. "On the Mathematical Foundations of Theoretical Statistics." *Philosophical Transactions of the Royal Society.* Series A. 222 (1922), 309-68.

9. ———. *The Design of Experiments.* Edinburgh, Oliver & Boyd, 1935.

10. Gauss, C. F. Letter to Olbers, Sept. 3, 1805. Quoted in G. W. Dunnington, *Carl Friedrich Gauss, Titan of Science.* New York: Exposition Press, 1955.

11. Grodins, F. S. *Control Theory and Biological Systems.* New York: Columbia University Press, 1963.

12. Milsum, J. H. *Biological Control Systems Analysis.* New York: McGraw-Hill Book Co., 1966.

13. Poincaré, H. *Science and Method*, trans. Francis Maitland. London: T. Nelson and Sons, 1914. Pp. 52-53.

What Are Mathematical
Models of Behavior Models of?[1]

Introduction

The form of the question suggests an answer (and a very
short paper). But behavior, even in its most narrow scientific
sense let alone in its ordinary, everyday meaning, is a grossly
misleading answer. If for no other reason, it is inadequate
because the social and behavioral sciences fail in any serious
scientific sense to treat the whole range of human behavior
and its concomitant emotional states, but more significantly,
it is inadequate because our models pertain only to a restricted class of the best formulated areas of these sciences
and, even there, they are only partially effective. Models of
behavior are our goal, not a claim of accomplishment. So the
question is not trivial. This does not mean that it is especially
subtle: any specialist can answer it readily for himself, although he may agree that it can be vexing to formulate it in
a way that communicates satisfactorily to his less mathematical colleagues. To a degree, the somewhat forbidding and demanding nature of mathematical discourse raises a barrier;

1. This paper was prepared while I was a National Science Foundation
Senior Postdoctoral Fellow at the Center for Advanced Study in the Behavioral Sciences, Stanford, California.

however, I suspect that the main difficulty is not the mathematics, but rather the scattered and none-too-systematic aspects of our present literature. If so, a system of classification may be of some help.

The scheme I use is neither deep nor entirely satisfactory. It fails many of the usual criteria for a good classification: the categories are neither sharply defined, exhaustive, mutually exclusive, nor do they form a simple hierarchy. The best I can claim for it is that the list is short enough to be remembered, that most models seem to fall reasonably comfortably into just one of the categories, and that I have failed to think of a better one. The six main headings are: models of variables (or, perhaps better, of attributes), simple models of phenomena, more complex models of phenomena, models of experiments, models of interactions among individuals, and models of social institutions and mechanisms. Throughout, I shall focus on behavioral and social processes and exclude all purely physiological and biological ones.

Models of Attributes

Physical scientists quickly become uneasy about the behavioral sciences when we fail to answer clearly the question: What are your fundamental variables and how do you measure them? Often this suggests to them that we have none that are uniquely ours (you may recall that an international commission once declared fundamental measurement to be impossible in psychology), in which case our sciences must be some admixture of applied biology, physics, genetics, etc. But such a conclusion flies in the face of common sense: all our talk of intelligence, love, hate, aggression, beauty, power, loudness, brightness, utility, and the like surely is not wholly idle. To deny the existence of such concepts because we currently do not know how to deal with them systematically is pseudo-scientific arrogance—what we can't formulate now can't be formulated—and to suppose that soon they will be reduced to terms from other sciences is simply scientific naïveté. We must assume that we speak, however imperfectly and vaguely, of something ultimately capable of careful analysis, just as 500 to 1,000 years ago men meant something close to what we now mean by concepts such as force, work, weight, length, heat, etc., even though they lacked satisfactory theories for any of them, could not measure many of them, even approximately, and partially misunderstood all of them.

Aside from subjective scaling in psychophysics (loudness, brightness, etc.), the careful theoretical analyses of utility stemming originally from economics and statistics, and the none-too-satisfactory but widely used attempts to measure abilities and intelligence, psychology as a whole has tried to bypass the problem of analyzing its variables by substituting so-called physical indicators or indices for them. We really wish to control and manipulate hunger, but instead we control and manipulate hours of deprivation. It is doubtful that they are monotonically related, but, what is worse, we tend to drop hunger from our kit of scientific concepts in order to be entirely, if a bit inappropriately, operational. We wish to control and manipulate aversiveness, but instead we control and munipulate milliamperes of current. And on and on. The simple fact is that we do not yet understand the structure of most of the attributes we believe affect and accompany behavior, and so we substitute for them what we hope are partially correlated physical measures that we do understand.

Rather than deny our variables, we must learn how to isolate and purify them, to measure them, and to relate them one to another in systematic theories. One class of behavioral models is addressed to this task. It is probably the least understood and least popular of our efforts, but it is doubtful if much of great generality is possible in the behavioral sciences until some of these problems are cracked.

The first sign that a serious examination of an attribute has started is the appearance of empirical exchange relations for that attribute. An exchange relation simply tells what may be substituted for what without altering the amount of the attribute exhibited. At the very least, this requires some means to decide whether two entities—stimuli, events, outcomes, etc.—exhibit the attribute to the same degree, and often it is useful to be able to order the entities according to which has more of the attribute. One cannot say a priori how this is to be done; indeed, discovering a qualitative method for ordering them according to the attribute is usually the heart of the problem. At present, psychologists frequently depend upon a subject's judgment: he tells us which outcome he prefers, which tone seems louder to him, which event he believes to be more probable, etc. Whether more refined and stable methods can be evolved remains to be seen.

However the data may be obtained, the model-builder then attempts to isolate properties—consistent patterns that reflect constraints imposed by the subject—that are (approximately) true for all subjects (of some population). If he uncovers enough of these properties, he may then be able to establish some sort of representation (usually in the real numbers or in an Euclidean n-space) that provides a compact summary of the data and a method for making ready deductions about them. The representation is merely a convenience (albeit, a considerable one); the substance of the theory is not the representation, but rather the qualitative properties that have been found in the data.

Two general types of exchange relations have been studied.

In the first, the attribute is manipulated simply by forming combinations of entities where both the entities and their combinations exhibit the attribute; physical mass and length are prototypes. Various consistencies are observed, which in the case of mass may be summarized by the ordinary representation: to each object a number, called its mass, is assigned in such a way that numerical inequality reflects the qualitative ordering determined by, say, an equal-arm pan balance, and the mass of a collection of objects is numerically equal to the sum of their individual masses. Little has been done with this particular theory (of extensive measurement) in psychology, but somewhat similar theories have been proposed for the bisection of pairs of stimuli in psychophysics and for the measurement of utility (HBMP, 1, 6, 19).[2]

In the second type of exchange relation, two or more independent variables each affect the same attribute and the exchange is a statement of how much one of the independent variables has to be altered to compensate for a given change in another. A physical example is momentum (the attribute) and the exchange is between mass and velocity (the independent variables). An economic-psychologic one is utility (the attribute) and the exchange is among amounts of difference commodities or, in expected utility theory, between commodities and the probabilities of receiving them. The utility exchange relation is called an indifference curve. Many exchange relations, usually called equal-name-of-attribute curves, are known from psychology: the exchange between frequency and intensity to maintain equal loudness of pure tones, between amount and delay of reward to main-

---

2. All references are to chapters of Luce, R. D., Bush, R. R., and Galanter, E. *Handbook of mathematical psychology*. Vols. 1-3. New York: John Wiley and Sons, 1963-65. There are indicated by HBMP followed by the chapter number. Numerous more detailed references are given there.

tain equal incentive, between hit and false alarm rates to maintain equal detectability (ROC curves), between resistance and voltage to maintain equal aversiveness of shock, etc.

A family of detailed algebraic theories, known collectively as conjoint measurement theories, is being developed as a set of possible formal structures within which to analyze exchange relations of this sort. Perhaps the best known examples are expected utility theory and additive conjoint measurement (HBMP, 19).

Because the subjects' responses often are inconsistent in some way, the algebraic theories are not always easy to apply. To overcome this difficulty, a variety of probabilistic models, more-or-less closely related to the algebraic ones, are also being elaborated (HBMP, 19). Characteristically, they postulate, among the response probabilities, constraints which go beyond those of probability theory itself. Sometimes, although by no means always, a numerical scale similar to those in the algebraic theories is either assumed or deduced, and the probabilities depend upon those scale values in some systematic way.

Simple Models of Phenomena

Aside from attributes which adhere to stimuli, responses, and outcomes, and for which ordering concepts seem appropriate, there are many behavioral events that are best thought of as discrete, qualitative phenomena. A stimulus is or is not detected, a problem is or is not solved, an association is or is not learned, an item is or is not remembered, a decision is or is not taken, etc. To be sure, in many cases some notion of degree may also be appropriate: a stimulus may be detected with some degree of confidence or with some probability, a problem may be solved partially, an association may be learned gradually or with some probability, an item may be remembered partially, or a decision may be taken with a certain dispatch. Nevertheless, a distinction between attributes and occurrences seems useful, even though any model of a phenomenon, such as for the detection of stimuli or for learning, will usually have a place in it for the attributes of the stimuli, responses, and outcomes that contribute to the phenomenon.

Unlike the models for variables, which merely state low level abstractions from the observable data, those for phenomena are usually cast in terms of hypothetical happenings as well as in terms of observables. They explicitly acknowledge a conceptual structure within the organism—not the moist red and grey structures of the physiologist, but a hypothetical one of representations of stimuli, of storage and decay, of associations and random sampling, of counting mechanisms, and of elementary comparisons and decisions. It is a simple internal world, composed of processes simpler than those built into even the most primitive digital computer, but one whose consequences, which generally are worked out in considerable detail by mathematical methods, often are of the same order of complexity as the experimental data now available.

A few well-known examples serve to illustrate this type of model. Several models for psychophysical detection and recognition (HBMP, 3) postulate that each stimulus leads to an internal representation that we can treat as a random variable (with values in the continuum of real numbers in the Thurstone and closely related signal detectability models and in a discrete set of numbers in the threshold models). The subject is assumed to partition the set of possible values into classes that he makes correspond to possible response alternatives, and the boundaries of the partition are affected in systematic ways by other experimental variables such as payoffs and presentation probabilities. The random variables and the partitionings are, of course, unobservable.

Stimulus sampling theory of learning (HBMP, 10) supposes that an unobservable set of elements partially reflects something of the stimulus conditions of the experiment, that each element is conditioned in some way to one or another of the possible responses, and that the decision as to which response to make on a given trial is reached by counting in a random sample the number of elements that are conditioned to different responses. Following the response and outcome, the conditioning of some of the elements may be changed. Models of this general type are sometimes called urn schemes, and they have been postulated for a variety of psychological processes.

Lately there has been a resurgence of interest in short term memory which has led to a number of clever experiments and several plausible, if difficult to test, models. Among the hypothetical phenomena embodied in the models are abstract, somewhat imperfect representations of the stimuli, temporary storage during which information about the order of arrival of stimuli may be lost, decay in the representations, and various forms of elementary decision-making.

It is no exaggeration to say that the sizable majority of all psychological models are of this general type. At least four reasons underlie their popularity. First, the phenomena in question are undoubtedly important and have been so thought throughout the history of psychology. Second, considerable data are already available, and well established experimental paradigms make it relatively easy to collect additional data that are pertinent to the models. Third, in spite of their unobservable constructs, these models usually predict observable, or nearly observable, behavior and so they bear on data quite directly. And fourth, such simple mechanisms are easy to think about and to formulate in familiar and comparatively elementary mathematics, although deriving conclusions from them can sometimes be quite a formidable task.

Such models as these exhibit two major difficulties, neither of which is necessarily insurmountable. First, the "observable" predictions of most are response probabilities that depend upon at least one, and often more, free parameters that must be estimated from data. The data are mostly, but not entirely (e.g., latencies), discrete responses. This incompatibility leads both to complex problems of estimation—often requiring more analysis than the model itself—and to subtle issues of evaluation when we try to decide if the model is adequately consistent with the data. Second, as one passes from models for the simplest experiments—usually those with one or two stimulus conditions and one or two responses—to more complicated ones, the model-builder faces a multitude of decisions about what is supposed to be going on in the "mind" of his hypothetical subject. Since none of these postulated processes can be observed directly and since often it is not readily apparent how different choices affect the predictions, one usually begins to feel as if he has entered into a never-never land of choices. This may lead him to turn experimenter and to undertake an elaborate, time-consuming series of studies designed to ferret out each choice point more or less independently of the others. Although progress can be made along these lines—the work in discrimination learning is a good example—it is usually very painstaking. Perhaps the most vivid example of these conceptual difficulties and the corresponding attempts to isolate different subprocesses is to be found in the current work on short-term memory.

The obvious, and possibly the only, alternative tack is direct physiological observation of what are now hypothetical processes. Were this possible, the development of these models would be greatly accelerated. I doubt, however, that we have much hope of aid from this quarter in the near future. The level of abstraction of the events postulated in the models does not seem to correspond at all well with the phenomena that physiologists are now able to isolate. Of course, physiological psychology has seen a number of impressive developments in the past two decades and is changing rapidly, so perhaps we will be surprised, but it would be unwise to count on it.

To close the section, a few words about the interrelation between models of attributes and phenomena are appropriate. Models of phenomena almost always end up with free numerical parameters that must be estimated from data, and sometimes the parameters seem to have a natural, intuitive interpretation as numerical scales of one sort or another—of stimulus intensity, utility, learning rate, etc. Thus, in principle and occasionally in practice (e.g., signal detectability theory), models of phenomena provide indirect scales of attributes. This fact has not been as effectively exploited as one might have hoped. Such scales, if worked out in detail, should provide significant hints to the measurement theorist about the types of scales needed and their dependence on experimental variables. In the opposite direction, as measurement improves, it should become possible to incorporate direct measurements into the theories of phenomena, thereby reducing or eliminating the free parameters. Nothing along this line has yet been done.

More Complex Models of Phenomena

Although the logical distinction between simple and more complex models of phenomena is fuzzy, two simple operational criteria suffice at the moment. We say that a model is of the more complex category if either it is too complex to be stated mathematically and is only formulated as a computer program or if it is one that involves several intermediate processes which have been studied in some detail by themselves. A few words about each type will suffice.

In computer simulations of decision-making and learning (HBMP, 7), the "mind" of the hypothetical subject is embodied in a computer program which is analogous to the mathematical models of phenomena, but is vastly more complex. The innumerable choice points of a program, with its possibilities for complex comparisons and detailed combinatorial explorations, far exceed in complexity anything that one would be willing to formulate mathematically. Which choices to make, when so many exist, seems beyond any hope of sensible resolution; yet those who have written such programs seem to hold that this freedom is illusory. One has to be a bit ingenuous to believe this claim which, I suspect, either reflects some over-enthusiasm for the method or a failure to acknowledge the numerous implicit choices that have been made. Some of these choices are probably buried in the programming language that happens to be used. The problems in evaluating these models are at least as severe as for the mathematical ones. Some programs predict specific responses on each trial (of course, it is trivial to modify them so that they do not), in which case we surely do not want to reject a program on the basis of one erroneous prediction. If not one, how many? Since subjects do do different things, how do we alter the program to handle their differences? These and related issues of evaluation have not been dealt with very effectively in the literature.

Our second class of more complex models includes those concerned with specific peripheral sensory processes, mainly in the eye and the ear, for which it is possible to get detailed physiological, mechanical, and chemical information about various of the steps (HBMP, 15, 16). The models describe the transduction of energy through these organs. An attempt is made to take into account data obtained at each interface, thereby reducing appreciably the number of unguided choices that have to be made. The resulting over-all models, which often are quite complex, are remarkably good in describing even the fine detail of the transduction. As we noted, similar methods are not currently available when we are concerned with phenomena that occur in the central nervous system.

Models of Experiments

Since the models just discussed are of interest only to the extent that they pertain to experiments, they could all be classed as models of experiments. But I don't mean that. Rather, I refer to models that are relatively atheoretic, that apply to just one or to a very limited class of experiments, and that are, to be blunt, little more than an elaborate form of curve fitting. The last charge is not likely to be well received by the authors of such models.

The attempt—admittedly not as successful as one would like—in the models previously discussed is to isolate and describe phenomena that take place within the organism and that in some way constrain his possible behavior. From these postulates we deduce what such a hypothetical organism will do when confronted with the boundary conditions established by this or that particular experiment. The idea is to parallel the approach taken in classical physics in which certain (usually differential) equations describe the constraints that hold among physical variables in all situations, and any particular situation is specified by boundary conditions for the equations. Together, the boundary conditions and the equations lead to specific predictions for the particular situation. Such a division into theory and boundary conditions has proved an extremely powerful technique since having once evolved the theory a model may, in principle, be constructed for any new situation provided only that it is adequately described. Something like that, feeble though it may be in comparison to what is done in physics, is being attempted, for example, in detection theory, in stimulus-sampling theory, and in the work on memory.

A model of an experiment may be defined negatively: it is one that fails to separate clearly the postulated properties of the organism from the boundary conditions that represent a particular situation (experiment). At present, most if not all of our work fails to some degree to make this separation and so, to that degree, our models are of experiments; but some are considerably more satisfactory than others. Much of the work using linear and nonlinear stochastic operators and Markov chains (HBMP, 9, 10) to analyze simple learning data suffers badly from this failure of separation. If one of these models accounts well for one experiment, we rarely know what to predict about a closely related one: there is insufficient underlying theoretical structure to venture much beyond what we already know.

Atheoretic models may, of course, be extremely valuable in predicting (extrapolating) things of practical importance. The input-output models of various industries and national economies is one example. When, however, the models are for experiments whose only conceivable interest is the possible insights they may give into basic phenomena, their usefulness is less clear.

Models of Interactions among Individuals

Were our models of individuals adequate, models for their interactions would, in principle, be easily constructed. All of the other individuals would form part of the (time-varying) boundary conditions of any one, and it would be a purely mathematical (or, more likely, computational) problem to deduce predictions. Judging by the troubles physicists have had in solving the equations for small numbers of interacting particles, the working out of these deductions would be dreadfully difficult. Although this approach seems somewhat fanciful at our present level of development, limited examples actually exist: Markov learning models to describe two individuals interacting in a simple game-like situation, several computer simulations of interacting individuals, and game theory in which each individual is assumed to make a rational analysis of the rational behavior of the others which, together with their individual utility functions, sometimes lead to (prescriptive) decisions (HBMP, 14).

Since, however, this approach is not yet suited to the analysis of most small group processes of interest, other authors have attempted to abstract various global aspects of interacting groups and to construct models in these terms. In one type of model (HBMP, 14), the group is assumed to be described in terms of time-varying variables such as pressure to communicate, cohesion, and the like, and certain differential equations are assumed to interrelate the variables. The properties of these equations have a certain intuitive plausibility, but the fact of the matter is that little can be done to test them since no one has the slightest idea how such variables should be measured. In another type of model (HBMP, 14) the time course and many other details of the interaction are abstracted away until all that remains are certain discrete structural links between some pairs of individuals. Depending upon the focus of interest, they may represent lines of authority, possible communication channels, affective relations, etc. The hope is that the structure of these graphs, as they are called, will reveal something of the social psychology involved. Many mathematical properties of these structures are known, and some of them (e.g., balance) are thought to correspond to socially important notions. It has, however, not proved easy to relate the mathematical definitions and theorems to empirical observations. Some of the difficulty may stem from the static nature of the abstraction, but probably more important is the fact that the abstraction does not really make any explicit assumptions about the participating individuals.

I think that it is safe to say that, so far, models of small group processes have contributed but little to our understanding of these processes. The fault does not, I think, lie with the model-builders, but with the basic intractability of the problem at the present time. On the one hand, there are no remotely adequate models of the individual behaving in a social environment and, on the other hand, there is no real opportunity to aggregate over sufficiently large collections of individuals so that statistical smoothing, as in some economic models, comes to our rescue.

Models of Social Institutions and Mechanisms

Although this category is quite extensive and includes some of the most successful models in the social sciences, I shall deal with it only briefly because the models do not refer to the behavior of individuals as such. Their basic terms are not individuals or their actions, but rather abstractions such as price, quantity, rate of interest, rate of growth, and so on. Of course, it is the actions of people that determine these variables, but the models make no attempt to analyze them from that point of view—and for good reason. The best examples are from economics, but somewhat similar ones are beginning to be developed in parts of sociology (e.g., for voting patterns within large groups of people) and in political science (e.g., some of the work on coalition formation).

I would class as similar the qualitatively quite different

models that use concatenation algebras and the theory of recursive functions to analyze the underlying grammatical structure of languages (HBMP, 11, 12, 13). Here the basic terms are linguistic rather than economic or behavioral. It is possible that such models will come to play a significant role in the development of theories of behavior since universal aspects of languages undoubtedly reflect certain deep-seated human constraints. In particular, the study of language learning and concept formation should be affected.

Concluding Remarks

Of the above categories, only the ones for attributes and phenomena include models directly concerned with the behavior of individuals. Other models may well bear upon behavior, but the core of mathematical psychology is in these two areas. Confining our attention to them, it may be useful to conclude by citing a few of their present failings.

Work in the theory of measurement has not yet begun to make clear how many inherently different variables there are. If one is to judge by the scaling of psychophysical attributes, the number is fantastically large; however, I suspect that this is much like treating the energy of chemical reaction A as a measure distinct from the energy of B. Even though the modalities involved are inherently different, could it be that there is a single notion of subjective intensity of which, for example, loudness and brightness are just two special cases? For this to be possible, a subject should be able to say whether a given sound is more or less intense than a given light, which at first hearing sounds pretty silly. Yet experimentalists using the method of cross-modality matching have found that subjects can do just this and that they do it consistently. So, perhaps, ultimately there will be a grouping of some attributes into a single theory of measurement of subjective intensity.

Similarly, there appears to be a group of attributes that can all be called affective. Already, economists have been willing to group together all sorts of disparate economic goods under the common affective measure called utility. To extend this sort of measurement to other things that we like and dislike in varying degrees, such as shocks and other stimuli used as reinforcers, may be possible. It should be noted that many stimuli can be viewed as possessing both intensity and affect, and so at least two types of measures are associated with them.

A third general class of measurements that seems to hang together are those that may be called predictive and for which some sort of probability concept is the common attribute. Here the unity seems already to have been achieved, and one has no hesitancy in comparing events of quite different types by the same measure.

How many other categories of measurement will be needed is unclear; it is doubtful whether some of the personality concepts, if they can be measured at all, fall among these three. Nevertheless, considerable simplification will have been achieved if it can be shown that many apparently distinct attributes are special cases of a single variable and can be measured on the same scale.

Turning to models of phenomena, two limitations are striking. First, the models are mostly concerned with choices (or decisions) from prescribed sets of (basically, non-verbal) responses, and with the effect of input information, rewards, and risk on these choices. At least part of the reason for this limitation is the use of probability theory which strongly invites the choice formulation, but whatever the reason, the result is that much of importance has escaped the model-builder. We do not make choices every instant. When do we view situations as partitioned into alternatives? Why do we partition them as we do when we do? In part, this must be related to certain perceptual problems of how energy distributions over time are structured into unitary concepts such as people, chairs, etc. How do we create these concepts and how can they be modified? What is the nature and role of various emotional states? How do motor skills develop and what influences their acquisition? And so on. The point is simple; choices, although important, are really only a small part of our behavior and it is unlikely that they will be well understood without at least some understanding of other aspects of behavior.

A second, and related, limitation is that both the models and the experiments involve a vast amount of repetition of the same or nearly the same choice situation, usually structured in the form of discrete trials. The reason for this is that the models talk about probabilities but the experiments provide choice data, and only by making repeated observations can we estimate probabilities from data. Since these experiments are a far cry from any natural environment of the subjects, animal or human, one cannot help being a bit edgy about just what it is that we are studying. If learning requires one hundred or more identical trials, what organism would ever have the opportunity to learn in his usual environment? I believe that it is important that we try to break out of some of these self-imposed limitations, although I confess I do not see clearly how to do it.

When Does a Model
Represent Reality?

It would be both foolish and boring were I to summarize the richness of this symposium by a listing of its main events. A more obvious choice for me to make is to show how each speaker was concerned with a client he wished to satisfy and thus to relate the whole to the concern of my paper.

Consider the following assertions of the authors:

> The student of model-building seeks the answer to the question: how does one analyze a set of real events in order to isolate and define the important variables that appear to be operating? (Stogdill)

> I think it is safe to say that, so far, models of small group processes have contributed but little to our understanding of these processes. The fault lies with the basic intractability of the problem at the present time. There are no remotely adequate models of the individual behaving in a social environment. (Luce)

> It gradually dawned that the Inter-Nation Simulation was a theoretical construction being complemented by the verbal and mathematical work which had been incorporated into an operating model. (Guetzkow)

> I would like to start from the basic fact that every model, of a real system, is in one sense second rate. Nothing can exceed, or even equal, the truth and accuracy of the real system itself. (Ashby)

A major skill required of students in the social sciences is a basic ability to abstract from reality to a model. Problems in the social and behavioral sciences are prima facie enormously complex. (March)

The process of model development may be usefully viewed as a process of enrichment or elaboration. One begins with very simple models, quite distinct from reality, and attempts to move in evolutionary fashion toward more elaborate models which more nearly reflect the complexity of the actual management situation. (Morris)

What inference can be drawn from the sample? With the biased interpretation of a philosopher, I'd say the inference is that model-builders have a healthy respect for reality. Mr. Luce thinks we're some distance from "it." Mr. Stogdill wants students to work from "it." Mr. Guetzkow began to see that his simulation was not more "it" than a theoretical construct is "it." Mr. Ashby says "it" has a truth and accuracy that no model can attain. Mr. March wants social science students to abstract from "it." Mr. Morris wishes his students to approach "it" cautiously, by a gradual elaboration.

Now if the model-builders are the client, it is clear that we should understand this common concern of theirs about reality. If Mr. Stogdill and Mr. March want students to make models of reality, what do they mean by this stipulation? What is the real social group process, international system, or physical world?

Philosophers, of course, have discussed this matter endlessly. Being prone to paradox, they have pointed out that reality must be and must not be a mental construct. It must be a mental construct, because otherwise it's unintelligible. It must not be a mental construct, because otherwise reality is all mental, which is silly.

But if we were to ask the question about reality in the spirit of serving the client, then perhaps the philosophical issue need not become so damnedly sticky. What is it that these model builders want to do? They want to abstract from reality, or map reality, or model reality realistically. They believe there is something called the real world which is very complicated and largely unknown. Their wish is to get students or themselves to model this reality as well as may be.

Still, the client hasn't succeeded in saying what it is he wants to do. He can't seriously mean he wants to map reality into a model unless he can tell us what is being mapped. But if he can tell us *that*, what does he need models for at all?

But the idea of "client" does suggest a clue. Suppose someone comes into your well stocked shop and says, "I want an oregue to spanilize the franfran." You understand the beginning of the sentence, but the rest is mystifying. However, you don't want to lose a well-heeled client. You ask him to explain, but he keeps talking in a frustrating manner: "An oregue is not a franfran, but it can be made to spanilize a franfran; answer me, do you have one that does this?" Now if you're wise you'll begin trying some things, and at first he'll say, "Not that, for heaven's sake: that doesn't spanilize *anything!*" But after a bit, you'll develop a model for this customer. The model will suggest some items to try, and he'll admit you're getting closer. Finally, he may say, "That's it! There's an oregue that really does spanilize the franfran." At that point you might have some idea of what your client really did want.

Of course this example must seem unfair. Everybody understands so well what reality is, because the feeling of reality is a deep-seated psychological force. Hence the idea of "representing reality" by a model is also well understood. But it is this very fact of common understanding which makes the client's wishes so hard to satisfy in this case. Since everyone knows so well what it means to represent reality, no one is willing or able to articulate his demand. It is as though we had traveled the circle of meaning; the empty "an oregue to spanilize the franfran" and "a model to represent reality" turn out to be very close in terms of their meaningful content.

Well then, shall we say that a model represents reality when the client is satisfied that it does? Should Mr. March give A's to the students who are satisfied that they've modeled reality? Why is Mr. Luce so dissatisfied, even though other more optimistic model-builders are quite satisfied? Mr. Ashby tells us he'll never be satisfied, that there's a limit to the shop's inventory, and even though we used every item we'd never find an oregue to spanilize the franfran. Mr. Guetzkow ends his paper by admitting he'd at best found only a "crude approximation" at considerable effort over ten years, a very rusty oregue to be sure. He hints that this search for a realistic model left him far less satisfied than were some of his complacent colleagues in safer disciplines. But despite his dissatisfaction, he feels that his search for a model has produced something more realistic than the models of more complacent students of international negotiation.

No, satisfaction alone cannot be what the client wants; when the satisfied customer gets home he may be furious to find that the item doesn't fit his needs at all. What is needed is some "quality control." Specifically, the product needs to be tested under severe conditions. All of which means that the client will be really satisfied if all the strongest efforts have been made to show that the product is defective. In the case of our client, he will really be satisfied when all the strongest efforts have been made to show that his model is deceptive, and it survives these efforts.

Here we have an operational definition of "reality," or more precisely, of our client's wish to "abstract the relevant characteristics of the real system." A model will be said to be an adequate abstraction if it meets the severest challenges that qualified minds can raise.

Does this operational definition help? It does suggest to Mr. March and Mr. Stogdill that a course in model-building should assign devil's advocates for each student's proposed model. It does clarify Mr. Luce's and Mr. Guetzkow's optimistic depression. They imply that the set of challenges that can be addressed to the model and its builder cannot be adequately answered at the present time, and, for Mr. Ashby, never. Mr. Morris, while being clever enough to avoid talking about the realism of models, does emphasize very well the challenges, and most especially the "ease of enrichment"; one of the most severe challenges one can make of a model is to insist that its designer try to elaborate beyond his originally intended scope.

Finally, the operational definition of reality seems helpful because it does clarify one very confusing issue about model-building. If reality is taken as a fixed entity, "out there," or as residing in fixed observational facts, then the model-builder's task is to find a model that comes as close to representing this fixed state of affairs as possible, or as his limited resources permit. Reality, in this case, sits there passively, waiting to be represented.

But if reality is the set of all relevant challenges of the model, then it is no longer passive. It is, in fact, a set of very creative acts, themselves based on a model. The task of the challenger of a model is to build a model that will most fiercely challenge. "Facts" are the result of observation-plus-model, because an observation must always be interpreted, and if an astute challenger can find a clever method of interpretation, he can create a reality that will adequately destroy a model.

All this amounts to saying that the model-building client creates his own dissatisfaction. To paraphrase Kant, reality would not be so immense and complicated had not the client made it that way. But in this commentary, I have been borrowing from a more recent writer, from the story of reality that E. A. Singer recounts in his *Experience and Reflection*. Reality, says Singer, is the repository of all unanswered questions. Psychologically, it is the fountain of all intellectual challenges. If the fountain dries up, the intellect dies. The fountains of the intellects of those who wrote these papers are very full.

Problems in Model-Building

Introduction

A large share of the creative excitement in contemporary social science is linked to the adventures of defining, applying, and testing analytical models of human behavior. As a result, we will be considering some things of current interest to research workers in social science. But the tools are not solely for the "professionals." They should be a part of the repertoire of any interested citizen concerned with understanding the behavior of man in society.

The models to be considered are some of those used most frequently and most generally in modern social science—anthropology, economics, geography, political science, psychology, and sociology. The primary emphasis is on developing skills in applying a few relatively simple concepts to problems in predicting, understanding, and influencing individual and collective human behavior.

Although the approach is a common one among social scientists, it differs from the implicit assumptions of some social science teaching and possibly from the reader's previous experience or expectations. He should be aware of these major differences:

1. The basic mode is one of abstracting from reality rather than attempting to represent the full complexities of human behavior.

2. The objective is skill in using the concepts rather than knowledge of specific factual material.

3. The flavor is pre-mathematical in the sense that although no mathematics (beyond high school algebra) is used, the models outlined are in a form amenable to formal mathematical treatment.

We shall consider five basic models—or at least the analysis of human behavior in five different situations:

1. *Individual choice.* The processes by which individuals choose, make decisions, and solve problems are processes of persistent interest to students of human behavior. Investment behavior, gambling, voting, occupational choice, consumer behavior, and the selection of mates are a few of the many choice situations that are of interest in their own right.

2. *Collective choice.* Frequently we are interested in the ways in which collectivities of individuals reach mutually satisfactory joint decisions. Communities, groups, organizations, societies resolve conflicts and make choices.

3. *Exchange.* One standard, and very pervasive, device for collective choice is exchange. Classical exchange of economic goods in the market place is one example, but there are others. The exchanges involved in the cold war, in small groups, in marriage, in political coalition formation also are subject to analysis through an exchange model.

4. *Adaptation and change.* Individuals and collectivities modify their behavior over time in response to experience. Whether we are considering learning, personality development, socialization, organizational or cultural change, or deliberate attempts to modify behavior, we require a model of adaptation on the part of the individual or collectivity.

5. *Diffusion.* A casual look at human behavior suggests that behaviors, attitudes, knowledge, and information spread

through a society. Sometimes they seem to spread slowly, sometimes rapidly. Fads, fertilizers, rumors, political attitudes, and new products are some of the specific things in which we might be interested. We wish to be able to predict the rate and pattern of their diffusion.

Problem Set 1 is a preliminary introduction to the basic style of the course. Subsequent problem sets are related more directly to the major sections of the course.

PROBLEM SET 1

1. Mr. and Mrs. Dewright have three sons: Manfred, Albert, and Chauncey. Manfred, the oldest, is a dutiful and loving son, doing his chores with dispatch. Albert, the second oldest, is seemingly co-operative but manages to avoid doing most of his chores. Chauncey, the youngest, is likely to have a tantrum whenever he is asked to do some work.

What are the problems in explaining these differences? Outline two explanatory models of individual differences and indicate how you would choose between them.

2. The Registrar at California Atlantic University has reported the following results from his preliminary study of changes in student majors during the freshman year at CAU: "If we compare the choice of major field made by students at the start of the freshman year with the choice made at the end, we seem to find that the ratio of men to women *increased* in each department of the university. However, at the same time, the overall university ratio of men to women *decreased*. That is, all departments became more 'masculine' while the university as a whole became more 'feminine.'"

Is the Registrar clearly confused? Outline a model that would explain such a phenomenon. How plausible is it?

3. Each year in the United States a large number of high

school seniors decide to apply to a college (or colleges) of their choice. The United States Commissioner of Education would like to be able to (a) predict, and (b) influence these application decisions. How would you develop a reasonable model for him to use? What kinds of additional information would be useful to you? What problems would you foresee?

4. In the "World Series" of baseball, the champion team of the American League plays a series of games with the champion team of the National League. They play until one team has won four games. The first team to win four games is called the "World Champion." The editor of *Sporting News* has raised the following questions: (a) Does the better team always win? (b) Is the better team more likely to win?

How would you answer such questions?

Individual Choice

Individuals are constantly making choices, but are perhaps not always aware of the fact that choice is involved. The following problems illustrate kinds of real life situations for which models of choice behavior can be developed.

PROBLEM SET 2

1. The Mesa Court Casino offers two tables for its patrons:
   Table 1: The patron pays $1.00 to play. A coin is flipped twice. The house pays $1.00 for each "head" that appears.
   Table 2: The patron pays $10.00 to play. Two coins are flipped. If they are both the same, the patron is allowed to play free at Table 1 for fifteen plays.

If the patrons are rational, what will they do?

2. Suppose seat belts cost $10.00 and that they cut the probability of being killed in an auto accident in half. Suppose also that last year in the United States 50,000 people (out of a population of 200,000,000) would have been killed in these accidents if no one had worn a seat belt.

   a. How much does a rational man's life have to be worth before he will buy a seat belt?

   b. Suppose a new seat belt were introduced that reduced the probability of a fatality to one-third its original value, and sold for $40.00. Who would buy it?

   c. Discuss what relevant considerations are omitted in this formulation of the problem.

3. Next month, there will be a major circus parade in the city. Herman Smith has obtained (for $50.00) the exclusive rights to sell sunhats and raincoats at the parade. Under the terms of his contract, he must sell sunhats at $.75 and raincoats at $2.00; but he can determine the number of hats and coats that he stocks.

From past experience with parades of this sort Mr. Smith knows that his sales will depend heavily on the weather. If the sun shines, he can sell 260 sunhats and 15 raincoats. If it is raining, he can sell 170 raincoats and 115 sunhats. If it is cloudy, he can sell 50 sunhats and 75 raincoats. The weather is fairly predictable. It rains about one day out of six; it is cloudy (but does not rain) about one day out of three; the sun shines the rest of the time.

Mr. Smith can obtain sunhats in 100 piece lots, and raincoats in 50 piece lots at the following prices:

SUNHATS		RAINCOATS	
100	$40.00	50	$15.00
200	70.00	100	30.00
300	90.00	150	40.00
		200	45.00

At these prices, the suppliers will accept no returns; any unsold merchandise must be dumped.

Assuming that Mr. Smith is rational, how many sunhats and how many raincoats will he stock?

4. The Fair Weather Forecasting Service of Costa Mesa can predict the local weather with certainty. The Service provides such predictions for a fee. If Mr. Smith is rational, how much should he be willing to pay for such a service?

5. The Santa Ana Medicine Man Corporation can control the local weather with certainty. If Mr. Smith is rational, how much should he be willing to pay for such a service?

6. Is it conceivable that two rational men would buy different automobiles? Specify the general circumstances (if any) under which such a thing could happen.

7. In what senses, and under what circumstances, can a "rational" man be said to have made the "wrong" choice?

PROBLEM SET 3

1. In the coming gubernatorial election, there are four alternatives:
   a. Vote for X
   b. Vote for Y
   c. Write in a vote for another candidate
   d. Do not vote

For *each* alternative, what is one set of consequences and criteria that would lead a "rational man" to select that alternative rather than one of the others?

2. Show how you would use such a rational model to predict each of the following statements *or its converse*:

a. Heavy voting (i.e., a high proportion of the eligible voters vote) is associated with close elections.

b. Close elections typically will have fewer write-in votes than will elections that are not closely contested.

c. The greater the difference between the programs of the two parties, the greater the proportion of eligible voters who will vote.

3. The university operates under an Honor Code. An Honor Code demands three things (among others):

a. That an individual not cheat on exams.

b. That he not permit another person to cheat.

c. That he report attempts to cheat.

Outline a model of rational student behavior and use it to predict:

a. When an individual would cheat.

b. When he would permit cheating.

c. When he would fail to report cheating.

4. According to your model in part 3 above, among which students would you expect greater Honor Code violations:

a. Among men or women?

b. Among good students or poor students?

c. Among resident students or commuters?

d. Among freshmen or sophomores?

Why?

5. If you were a student and wished to strengthen the Honor Code, what policies would you suggest to the University on the basis of your model?

6. Would a rational university have a big-time intercollegiate athletics program? Under what circumstances would you reach a different conclusion?

PROBLEM SET 4

1. In one of the assigned reprints, Davenport presents a game theory analysis of how a village should optimize its fish catch. Solve the same problem by assuming that a fisherman will seek to maximize expected value.

2. Each day in this country doctors make difficult individual choices in which they are asked by patients to prescribe birth control pills. In particular, the question arises with respect to prescribing for unmarried minor women without parental consent. Doctors operate under a code of ethics enjoining them to protect the health of their patients; they operate under a set of laws concerning the practice of medicine; they operate in a community with certain expectations about them.

    a. What policy would a rational doctor adopt in the situation as it exists locally?

    b. What could an individual patient do to modify that policy in the direction of making it more permissive with respect to prescription?

    c. What could an individual do to make the policy less permissive?

    d. Under what circumstances would you expect to find (in this case as well as more generally) a distinction between "official" and "unofficial" policy?

3. The Manila Conference has issued a statement suggesting possible conditions for peace in Viet-Nam.

    a. Assuming that Hanoi is rational, under what set of circumstances (i.e., alternatives and perceived consequences) would North Viet-Nam be willing to talk peace in such terms?

    b. Assuming that Washington is rational, under what

set of circumstances would the United States insist on the Manila terms?

c. Assuming that Hanoi, Saigon, Peking, Washington, and Moscow are individually rational, what are the prospects for peace in Viet Nam?

PROBLEM SET 5

1. George, Harry and Dick are seniors and must decide upon a career. They are crass materialists interested only in the money they can expect to earn in a profession. They are considering three alternatives and know what successful, average, and unsuccessful members of each profession earn:

	UNSUCCESSFUL	AVERAGE	SUCCESSFUL
Lawyer	$6,000	$12,000	$ 50,000
Business	3,000	10,000	100,000
Teacher	7,000	8,000	12,000

a. George figures his chances of being successful are about 10 per cent in law, 6 per cent in business, and 20 per cent in teaching. He estimates the risk of being unsuccessful at 30 per cent in law, 40 per cent in business, and 10 per cent in teaching. Assuming he is rational, which career will he choose?

b. Harry considers himself much brighter than George. "My chances of success in any career are certainly twice as good as George's," says Harry, "and my risk of failure must be only half as great." Since he too is rational, which profession can we expect him to choose?

c. Dick considers himself to be at least as rational as the next man. But he doesn't think that maximizing expected value is an appropriate way to go about making this decision. Why not? How else can he make his choice rationally? What career will he choose?

2. In each of the following situations indicate what choice a man would make if he is maximizing expected value:

a. *Alternate 1:* Roll a die. If a "one" appears, you win $12.00; otherwise you win $1.00 times the number of dots appearing on the face of the die.
Alternative 2: Flip a coin. If a head appears, you win $10.00; if a tail appears, you win nothing.

b. *Alternative 1:* Stay at home. You lose a sale ($40.00) but if it snows, you save the cost of a new fender ($150.00).
Alternative 2: Go out. You make a sale, but if it snows you lose a fender.

c. *Alternative 1:* Go to work. You can earn $5,000.00 the first year. This increases by $1,000.00 a year until it reaches $10,000.00, after which it is constant.
Alternative 2: Go to school. You pay $2,000.00 each year for four years. If you do not graduate (probability = 1/3), you earn $5,000.00 the first year after leaving school. This increases by $1,000.00 a year until it reaches $10,000.00 after which it is constant. If you do graduate, you earn $6,000.00 the first year. This increases by $1,000.00 a year until it reaches $11,000.00, after which it is constant.

3. A recent study for the Republican Party indicates the following effects of face-to-face contact during an election campaign.

a. If a Republican precinct worker contacts a registered Republican, he increases the probability he will vote from .5 to .6 and the probability that he will vote Republican from .8 to .9 .

b. If a Republican precinct worker contacts a registered
    Democrat, he increases the probability he will vote
    from .4 to .6 and the probability that he will vote
    Republican from .25. to .3 .

How would a rational Republican precinct worker behave?

4. Kim is studying Social Science 1 at Urvain College of
Idaho. He has learned three different methods of solving
problems, each of which requires one hour. The U.C. of I.
Social Science faculty has devised an hour exam consisting of
a problem which is a masterpiece of ambiguity. It may be a
problem of any of five kinds, and there is apparently no way
of telling without applying each method to see if it produces
an answer. The five kinds of problems are: (1) Method 2 always solves these, and method 3 solves 75 per cent of them;
(2) Method 1 always solves these, and method 3 solves 75
per cent of them; (3) Methods 1 and 2 solve 25 per cent of
these, while method 3 solves half of them; (4) Methods 1 and
2 solve these reliably, method 3 solves 75 per cent of them;
(5) Method 1 always solves these, method 2 solves half of
them, and method 3 solves 75 per cent of them.

a. If Kim evaluates the likelihood of each type of prob-
    lem as follows, A = 35 per cent, B = 25 per cent,
    C = 25 per cent, D = 10 per cent, E = 5 per cent;
    which method should he try?

b. If he knows the faculty desires him to have the high-
    est possible probability of failing, which method
    should he try?

5. If Paul Revere wished to minimize effort, under what
conditions would he say "two if by land and one if by sea"
rather than "two if by sea and one if by land"?

6. In *Action for Mental Health* by the Joint Commission
on Mental Health and Illness, there is a discussion of the

"Professional Manpower Dilemma." Their concern is mainly with the shortage of psychiatrists, general practitioners, psychologists, social workers, etc., but they also discuss the general professional manpower shortage in education, science, etc. A report by G. W. Albee (1959) states the following: "Of 10,000 youngsters in a given age group, 2,000 are in the top fifth with respect to intelligence; 1,963 of these enter high school, 1,857 graduate from high school, 864 enter college, and 692 graduate from college."

a.   Draw the "tree" representing this phenomenon: the explanation for the number of students who, after entering high school, fail to graduate from college includes (1) lack of interest; (2) lack of inspiration; (3) lack of self-discipline; (4) poor study habits; (5) lack of money.

If, in addition to being a separate factor, lack of money also contributes to the first four problems, then we might have a situation in which about half the problem is explained by a combination of things which might be called "motivation" and one half (in fact) explained by lack of funds.

If the manpower pool of the professions depends, to a large extent, "on the number of youths of superior mental competence who graduate from college and go on to graduate school," then a criterion for action would be: do those things which most help the largest number of persons needing help.

If an average input of $2,000 per dropout (in those cases where lack of money is the cause) would make the difference between graduating and not graduating from college, then:

b.   At the minimum, what should society (meaning the government and/or the professions themselves) be willing to contribute extra to the education of just

the top 1/5 of its youth? (Disregarding the amount
to the other 4/5 who may require even more persuasion to arrive at any point in the educational process.) NOTE: Assume that $\dfrac{692}{2000} = 1/3$.

7. There are many agricultural situations where expected
value calculations have practical value. For example, wine
grapes grow more valuable the longer they are left to grow.
But rain occurs late in the growing season and if the grapes
get wet they are completely ruined. Thus, the longer the
grapes are left to grow the greater the potential profit, but
the greater the chance of being wiped out by rain.

Unfortunately, grapes must be crushed within a few hours
of being picked; there are few wineries; crushing time must
be reserved long in advance; and so the decision of when to
harvest must be made by early August. In addition to choice
of harvest time, the farmer must also choose to "fully-crop"
or "under-crop" his land. Land that has been fully cropped
yields more grapes, and hence more profit, per acre. But
under-cropped land allows the grapes to ripen faster and be
picked sooner.

The following data apply:

PROFITS FROM GRAPE HARVESTS

Dates	Full-Crop Strategy	Under-Crop Strategy
Sept. 1-9	$ 50.00	$110.00
Sept. 10-19	80.00	130.00
Sept. 20-30	250.00	160.00
Oct. 1-9	320.00	160.00
Oct. 10-19	370.00	160.00
Oct. 20-30	400.00	160.00

a. Assume that the farmer has no knowledge of the
    probability of rain by any of these dates. What is the
    best minimax strategy for the farmer to pursue? That

is, what cropping and date combination will minimize the maximum harm that nature can do him?

b. One of the farmers has taken Social Science I and does a bit of research. He finds the weather has behaved as follows during the past:

PROBABLE WEATHER

Dates	Probability of rain	Probability of no rain
Sept. 1-9	.0	1.0
Sept. 10-19	.1	.9
Sept. 20-30	.2	.7
Oct. 1-9	.2	.5
Oct. 10-19	.2	.3
Oct. 20-30	.3	.0

Assuming that future weather will be the same what is his best plan now?

c. Assume that the new weather satellite will make possible perfect weather predictions. What is the value to the farmer of this additional information?

8. A rational man has the choice between the following two situations:

a. He can say "beer" and get Coors or Olympia with equal probability, or he can say "coffee" and get Maxwell House or Yuban with equal probability.

b. He can say "MO" and get Maxwell House or Olympia, or he can say "CY" and get Coors or Yuban, decided by a flip of a coin.

Which will he choose? Draw a short moral.

9. The Institute for Ulcer Detection is developing a two-test diagnostic procedure for detecting stomach ulcers along with treatment procedures.

Test A: This test costs $100 to administer. A patient

will exhibit a positive response to Test A about 60 per cent of the time.

Test B: This test costs $150 to administer. A patient will exhibit a positive response to Test B about 70 per cent of the time.

Furthermore, it is known that if a patient has a positive response on Test A, the probability is 83 1/3 per cent that he will have a positive response on Test B; if he has a negative response on Test A, the probability of a positive response on B is 50 per cent. Similarly, a patient with a positive response on B has a probability of 71.43 per cent of a positive response on A; if he has a negative response on B the probability of a positive response on A is 33 1/3 per cent.

There are three treatment procedures:

No treatment. This will "cure" the patient (with certainty) only if the response on both tests is negative. This treatment is free.

Diet. This will cure the patient (with certainty) if the response on no more than one test is positive. This treatment costs $200.

Drugs. This will cure the patient (with certainty) regardless of the test outcomes. This treatment costs $1,000.

None of the treatments or tests have adverse side effects. Assume that a doctor wishes: (a) To ensure that all patients will be cured. (b) To minimize the expected cost of curing them. What is the best test and treatment procedure (i.e., what tests and treatment should be given) to satisfy the doctor?

Collective Choice

Here, we will consider the analysis of collective choice. Where we previously attempted to study the processes by which individuals made decisions, we now turn to the ways in which individuals in collectivities—groups, organizations, societies—reach mutually satisfactory joint decisions. Among other things, we shall consider the problem of what constitutes a rational social choice. In this section we shall consider models of collective choice that are less concerned with exchange as a device for resolving conflict.

We shall examine collective choice from three points of view:

1. Rules for aggregating individual preferences as they affect the nature of the social choice.

2. A power model in which different individuals are seen as having different amounts of power over a decision.

3. Social devices by which people strive to increase the effectiveness of their power.

PROBLEM SET 6

1. Calculate the power of the individuals involved in each of the following situations. In each case indicate the model you are using and specific power values you calculate.

    a. Mr. Optimist used to think that 80 per cent of the world was nuts. Mr. Pessimist used to think that 45 per cent was. After some heated discussion, they each agree that the correct figure is 65 per cent.

    b. Mr. Adams argued before the Public Utilities Commission that the electric company should be given a rate increase of 5 per cent. Mr. Burns argued for 8 per cent. Mr. Chester suggested 3 per cent. The P.U.C. decided to give the company a 6 per cent increase.

c. Mr. Decisive wanted to go to the opera. Mrs. Decisive wanted to go to the ball game. They ended up going to the P.T.A.

2. How would you go about determining the relative power of the following people on a college campus?
   a. Dean of Students
   b. Vice-President for Business Affairs
   c. Dean of the College of Arts and Letters
   d. Professor of History
   e. President
   f. Vice-President for Academic Affairs
   g. Assistant Professor of Physics
   h. President of Student Association
   i. Typical sophomore

3. Suppose a political system consists of three groups, any two of which can form a winning coalition and then dictate governmental policy. Label these groups "Business," "Labor," and "Farmers." Suppose further that there are two policy decisions to be made: (a) Should industrial labor unions be subject to antitrust legislation? (b) Should new farmers be required to have college degrees in their specialty and be licensed by the government? Suppose finally that the Business Group is in favor of subjecting labor unions to antitrust regulation but is indifferent with respect to licensing of new farmers, that the Labor Group is opposed to antitrust legislation for unions but does not care whether new farmers are licensed, and that the Farmer Group has no strong feelings on antitrust but is in favor of licensing of new farmers.

What will happen in such a system? Outline the choice situation for each group and the way in which the situation would develop if we assumed rational choice behavior. Ignoring this particular example, is there a general proposition about coalition behavior in political systems that you can derive?

PROBLEM SET 7

1. The tables below indicate how individuals I, II, III, etc., rank (in order of preference) alternatives A, B, C, etc. For example, in the first table, individual I indicates that his first choice is alternative A, his second choice alternative B, etc. In each table, which alternative(s) are Pareto optimal?

(a)

	I	II
A	1	2
B	2	1
C	3	3
D	4	5
E	5	4

(b)

	I	II
A	1	5
B	2	4
C	3	3
D	4	2
E	5	1

(c)

	I	II	III	IV
A	1	1	1	3
B	2	2	2	4
C	3	3	3	5
D	4	5	4	1
E	5	4	5	2

(d)

	I	II	III	IV	V
A	1	1	1	1	5
B	2	5	2	2	1
C	5	2	3	3	2
D	3	3	4	5	3
E	4	4	5	4	4

(e)

	I	II
A	1	5
B	2	2
C	3	4
D	4	3
E	5	1

2. Legislation in the Federal Government can be passed in either of two ways: (*a*) by majority votes in the House of Representatives and in the Senate and a presidential approval; (*b*) by a two-thirds vote in each of the houses (after a veto by the president). The president wishes to maximize his influence over legislation. The present president would prefer a Democratic majority in both houses of Congress. The Congressional Democratic party, though not subservient to the president, is more sympathetic to his requests than is the Congressional Republican party.

    a. Assuming that each Congressional party is a homogeneous group with perfect party discipline, how large a Democratic majority should the president desire in order to maximize his own power? Why?

    b. Here is how the Congress looked before and after the 1966 election:

House	Before	After
Democrats	295	248
Republicans	140	187
Senate		
Democrats	67	64
Republicans	33	36

According to the model you used to answer part a, did the president's power over legislation increase, decrease, or remain the same as a result of the election?

    c. In fact, American legislative parties are rarely homogeneous. How would you modify your analysis to accomodate this fact?

3. The Berkeley administration has a policy which does not permit nonstudents to man tables for purposes of solicitation at the Sproul Hall Plaza. Recently, the Navy erected a recruitment stand on the plaza. Immediately following this,

another nonstudent (nongovernmental) stand was erected, which was quickly ordered to be taken down by the administration. A sit-in ensued, along with several student and nonstudent arrests. At present there is a semisuccessful boycott of classes going on, supported by some legitimate student groups, like the Teaching Assistant Union. Chancellor Heyns has thus far refused to negotiate with popular Mario Savio on the grounds that he is not a student. Governor-Elect Reagan, who will assume office in January, has informally made statements to the effect that the dissenting students had better "shape up or ship out."

a. Using a power model, what are the problems in predicting a final decision? Describe the sources and potential effectiveness of the power of Savio, Heyns, and Reagan.

b. Using your knowledge of the bargaining process, what are some of the variables that will determine the outcome of the dispute?

c. Make a prediction of what will happen in January, if the strike continues, and tell how you arrived at it.

4. The seats in the West German Legislature are distributed as follows: Christian Democratic Union (CDU), 245 seats; Social Democratic Party (SDP), 202 seats; and Free Democratic Party (FDP), 49 seats. The CDU-FDP governing coalition recently broke down. The crisis was resolved when the SDP, which has been the main opposition party since the establishment of the postwar federal government, joined in a coalition with the CDU. Why would they do that? Using one of your models of collective choice, what prediction could you make about the life expectancy of this government? Would you expect party discipline in the CDU and SDP to be easier or more difficult to maintain than before? How would you expect the FDP to behave?

The National Democratic Party (NDP), a neo-Nazi group, has no seats in the federal legislature, but showed surprising strength in the recent Bavarian state election. How would you expect the NDP to react to the new situation at the federal level?

Exchange

Situations in which exchange is either necessary or desirable (or both) are rather pervasive in a world of many, often conflicting, goals, and an understanding of the basic nature of exchange behavior is crucial.

Our major concern in this section is with developing the generalized model of economic exchange. We shall then see that the exchange model is, as was mentioned in our discussion of collective choice, intimately related to the choice models we have examined and, not surprisingly, that choice behavior and exchange behavior are related. Lastly, we shall examine both the empirical nature of the model and its application to a number of different kinds of actual problems.

PROBLEM SET 8

1. Suppose that we have measured the total utility of various quantities of apples and candy bars for Dan and found the following:

NO. OF APPLES	TOTAL UTILITY	NO. OF CANDY BARS	TOTAL UTILITY
0	0	0	0
1	10	1	50
2	19	2	55
3	27	3	59
4	34	4	62
5	39	5	64

   a. Draw the graph of total utility and marginal utility
       for apples and candy bars.
   b. Suppose that Dan now has five apples and three
       candy bars. How many candy bars will he want in
       order to give up one apple? What is his substitution
       ratio of apples for candy bars?

   2. Assume that Dan and Jim each have twenty candy bars
and twenty apples. With these initial amounts they have the
following substitution ratios: three candy bars equal one apple (Dan) and eight candy bars equal one apple (Jim).

   a. Compared to Dan, is Jim more found of apples or
       candy bars? How do you know?
   b. Can Dan and Jim engage in mutually beneficial
       trade? If so, can you tell anything about who will
       get what? If not, why?

   3. A parent gives each of his two children some meat and
some milk. The two children then exchange with each other,
one drinking most of the milk and the other eating most of
the meat. As a parent, would you permit them to make that
exchange?

   4. Assume that Joe has two dollars to spend on beer and
pretzels. Pretzels cost ten cents a bag, and beer costs twenty
cents a glass.

   a. Draw a graph with beer on the vertical axis and pret-
       zels on the horizontal axis, and draw in Joe's con-
       sumption possibility line.
   b. Assume that beer goes up to thirty cents a glass.
       Draw the new consumption possibility line.
   c. Do the same thing for a beer price of five cents.
   d. Assume Joe's budget doubles and that beer still costs
       twenty cents. Draw the consumption possibility
       line.

5.   "Two indifference curves cannot intersect each other." Explain why.

6.   If the consumer is at a point of his budget line (consumption possibility line) where it crosses an indifference curve, is he in equilibrium? If not, how should be move to maximize his utility?

PROBLEM SET 9

1.   Suppose Jim has ten units of food and five units of clothing, Dan has five units of clothing and ten of food, and their indifference maps are exactly alike. Is mutual trade between them likely to occur?

Suppose Jim and Dan each have ten units of food and five units of clothing, and suppose that their indifference maps are not exactly alike. Is mutual trade between them likely to occur?

2.   Exchange occurs not only among members of the same nation but also among members of different nations. Let's refer to David Ricardo's famous discussion of England and Portugal, recognizing that "England" is shorthand for "residents of England" and that "Portugal" is shorthand for "residents of Portugal." The labor hours required to produce a unit of cloth and wine in each country are:

	CLOTH	WINE
England	100	120
Portugal	90	80

a.   Will trade take place? If so, who will trade what?

b.   If trade occurs, what will the swapping terms be?

c.   Assume the exchange ratio is one unit of wine equals

one of cloth. Describe (in terms of labor hours saved) the division of the gains from trade.

d. Do you suppose that mutually beneficial trade is possible between the United States and Japan even though the Japanese wage rate is much lower?

3. Suppose there are seven stages in some production process. Each producer acts as an independent entrepreneur, performing his function and selling his product through an ordinary market transaction to the producer at the next stage. Suppose each producer spends seven hours per day in productive activity and one hour per day engaging in market activity, buying the output of producers at lower stages and selling his output to producers at higher stages. Note: One item passing through seven stages yields a finished product.

a. If each producer produces 100 items per hour, what is his cost of engaging in market activity (i.e., what does he give up in exchange for undertaking to sell his output and buy new inputs)?

b. What is the total cost, for the entire group, of using the market?

c. Suppose that some enterprising individual realizes than he could provide all administrative activity at a total daily cost of forty finished products. What sort of exchange will tend to take place?

d. What will be the range with which trade will tend to take place?

e. What important real world organization did Sir Dennis Robertson have in mind when he used similar considerations to explain why "islands of conscious power exist in this ocean of unconscious cooperation like lumps of butter coagulating in a pail of buttermilk"?

4. The concept of cost is derived directly from the implications of elementary exchange analysis; the cost of undertaking an activity is the alternatives that are given up. For example, the cost of a movie to you is the value of some other item you gave up in order to consume the movie. (This may be money, generalized purchasing power, but money itself derives most of its value from its ability to purchase other things).

  a. What is the cost of the personnel used to staff our armed forces, i.e., what is given up in exchange for employing these people in national defense?

  b. What does this exchange cost analysis imply about the validity of the allegation that if we were to replace the military draft, with its below-market-pricing, with a voluntary system the cost of national defense would be increased significantly? Why?

  c. It has been estimated that it would cost an additional $5 billion in military wages to do away with the current draft. What significance does this "cost" have for the relations between draftees and taxpayers?

PROBLEM SET 10

1. In the United States steel costs $100/ton and wheat costs $200/ton. In India steel costs 1,000 rupees/ton and wheat costs 4,000 rupees/ton. Assume the international monetary system has broken down and that all trade takes place through barter.

  a. Will trade take place? If so, in what direction?

  b. What will the swapping terms be?

2. Last week a U.C.L.A. professor said, "Education is ex-

pensive, but nothing is more valuable." Draw the implied indifference curves and budget lines. Is that statement correct?

3.   Newport Beach and Corona del Mar State Beach are "free public beaches." Is this true? What is their cost and who pays it?

4.   Assume that you were to work hard, practice smiling, learn to act, and some day become a state governor. Assume that your state has fifteen departments, lots of people, and not enough money. Specifically, its income is 10 per cent less than its planned expenditures. Popularity is very important to you and so you can't raise taxes. Question: How do you reduce expenditures? Your advisors suggest two possible ways: (a) Make a detailed examination of the budget of each department; cut out all those items which you believe are unnecessary, (b) Make an across the board 10 per cent budget cut by simply instructing each department to spend 10 per cent less money.

   a.   Which would you do? (Hint: use the analytic techniques we have given you in this course to learn how to be a better governor).
   b.   Suppose you believed that the work of some departments was more important than the work of other departments; or else, that even though the departments were all doing equally important work, that some were more efficient than others. Would this change your evaluation of the two methods for cutting expenditures?

5.   If Pussy Galore's marginal utility for more James Bond is high relative to her marginal utility for more Shakespeare, and if Honeychild Rider's marginal utility for more Shakespeare is high relative to her marginal utility for more James

Bond, explain what kind of trade can take place to make both Pussy and Honey happier.

Is the aggregate happiness (the sum of both their utilities) of Pussy and Honey, greater after the exchange than it was before?

Suppose that after the trade described above has taken place, Kissy Suzuki comes along and proposes a way to further increase the aggregate happiness of Pussy and Honey. Kissy argues that since Pussy has so much more of both James Bond and Shakespeare than Honey does, that Pussy should give up one unit of both goods to Honey; that this will only make Pussy a *little* bit unhappy, whereas the gain of one unit of both goods will make Honey *much* happier, and hence the aggregate happiness will be increased. Is this true?

Adaptation

This section will deal with the principles by which we adjust our behavior to changes in the environment. The final adjustment is viewed as a composite of other adjustments deriving from one's past experience and from demands of the physical or social context.

PROBLEM SET 11

1. Jerome, who is on a very tight budget, and his friend Kenneth both crave chocolate cake and cherry pie to an equal degree. Presented with a choice between these two desserts each day at the cafeteria, Kenneth decides immediately, while Jerome seems to take an eternity making up his mind. Why might this be, in terms of conflict principles?

2. Harold, ordinarily a pleasant companion, returns to the

dormitory after a dispute with his chemistry instructor and snaps at his friends, seeming to be "spoiling for a fight." What processes seem to be involved?

3.   Sue and Matilda are both "B" students, equivalent in intelligence, personality, and looks. Although they get about the same number of offers for weekend dates, Sue never accepts, preferring to stay home and study while Matilda goes out and has a good time (both are blondes). What kind of difference in parental training might they have received in regard to academic achievement?

4.   Mary can read French beautifully; the only problem is that she understands none of it. Spell out this missing factor in the language of conditioning.

5.   Alphonse has just eaten seven helpings of food at a banquet and is totally satiated. Having arrived home, he makes a beeline for the refrigerator and consumes four sandwiches. Apply the notion of "learned drive" to his behavior.

PROBLEM SET 12

1.   In attempting to teach a child to call a poodle by the name *poodle*, you point to it and utter repeatedly, *poodle*. Finally the child utters *poodle* whenever you point to the poodle.
   a.   Does the child now know what a poodle is?
   b.   How would you test to determine if he has the correct concept of the name *poodle*?
   c.   Can you think of a training procedure that would better insure that the child learned the concept of poodle as well as the name poodle?

2.   Professor Galois ran a little test on his four French I

sections. All four sections were given a list of the weekdays in English together with their French translations to study for five minutes. (The list was as follows: Sunday, *dimanche*; Monday, *lundi*; Tuesday, *mardi*; Wednesday, *mercredi*; Thursday, *jeudi*; Friday, *vendredi*; Saturday, *samedi*.) Sections 1 and 2 were instructed beforehand that their final test was going to be to give the French days correctly upon presentation of only the corresponding English days. Sections 3 and 4 were told that their test would be to give the English days to the French days alone.

Sections 1 and 3 were in fact tested as they expected. Sections 2 and 4, however, were tricked and tested in the reverse order from the order they had expected. The final results showed that Sections 2 and 3 each averaged seven correct, while Sections 1 and 4 averaged four correct.

a. Specify two kinds of learning and show how they can account for the differences between French sections.

b. Which sections seemed to have learned the most?

c. Which instructions seemed to have produced the most learning?

3. A conditioning experiment was conducted on two groups of subjects. Group 1 was highly motivated, while Group 2 was under low motivation. Both groups showed smooth learning curves over conditioning trials; but, while Group 1 leveled off at an asymptote of 80 per cent, Group 2 leveled off at an asymptote of 40 per cent. Each group approached its asymptote at the same rate.

When each group was divided into fast and slow learners, it turned out that while fast and slow learners leveled off at the same asymptotes, the slow learners approached the asymptote at a slower rate.

Assume that the response on any trial is a weighted average of the response on the immediately preceding trial and the asymptotic response. (Since the weights sum to one, use w and $1\text{-}w$ as the weights).

    a.   What are the parameters of the weighted average model?

    b.   Within the model, how do you represent the increment in response strength from trial n to trial $n+1$?

    c.   What do changes in the values of w and the asymptotic response reflect in terms of the experiment cited above?

4.   Three weeks before a party Kathy receives an invitation to it. She accepts. As the time for the party approaches, she becomes more and more restive. Finally on the night of the party she doesn't show up.

    a.   Formulate a simple model that might explain Kathy's conduct.

    b.   If you assume that many people behave like Kathy and you are having a party, when should you send the invitations out so as to receive as many acceptances as possible? As many rejections as possible? Make the answer in part b follow from the model in part a.

5.   You are observing two groups of children at a daycare playground. Their daily activities are being planned by the director. The children in Group A are being given the choice between a field trip to the countryside to see a cowboy ranch or else a trip to the beach to swim. Field trips take one day. The children in Group B are to remain at the daycamp all day and play games. They have a whole toy closet full of games, with many different kinds of each toy, and must decide which game to play first. Which group of children will

take the longest time to decide what it will do for its daily activities? Give a model along with your answer.

PROBLEM SET 13

1. "Absence makes the heart grow fonder." Set up a model and deduce from it the preceding quotation.

2. Sabrina dislikes liver as much as she does beets; she likes sherbet as much as she does peaches. Sabrina's mother announced the following menu for lunch: "Today we are going to have liver, beets, sherbet, and peaches." Thereupon, Sabrina flew into a tantrum and refused to eat.

The next week, her mother announced: "Today we are going to have peaches, sherbet, beets, and liver." Thereupon, Sabrina salivated heavily, and consumed the meal heartily and happily.

Assume that Sabrina's final evaluation of the meal was a weighted sum of her evaluation of the foods as announced to her.

    a.   How might you go about assigning weights so as to account for the difference between her reactions to the two menus? Give some psychological interpretation to your weights.

    b.   After finishing her meal, her mother asked her which of the foods she had most enjoyed, and which least. She replied that she liked the peaches most, and the beets least. With this further information, would you assign your weights differently?

3. An experimenter sets a half dozen egg cups before a six-year-old, which are arranged in a row with the same small spatial interval separating each adjacent pair. Directly opposite each cup he places an egg, and so they stand in one-to-one

correspondence. The child counts them easily, six eggs and six cups. Now the experimenter takes the cups and increases the interval between pairs, stretching out the set into a much longer line. The child is asked: "Are there as many cups as eggs? Are there more? Are there fewer?" The child replies: "There are more cups than eggs." When asked to recount the eggs and the cups, the child still maintains that there are more cups than eggs.

In fact, this is typical behavior for a six-year-old on this task. Can you account for this behavior on the basis of your knowledge of concept formation?

4.   There exist nine cards—three small ones, three middle-sized ones, and three large ones. One of the cards of each size is blue, one red, and one yellow. Lorna and Camille, five-year-olds, were separately trained to say *dog* upon presentation of the blue cards, *pat* upon presentation of the red cards, and *rip* upon presentation of the yellow cards. Both kids took twenty minutes to learn the test perfectly. Afterwards, on a new test, they were trained to say *mop* to the blue cards, *fin* to the red cards, and *sot* to the yellow cards. While Camille completed the task in five minutes, Lorna required thirty minutes to do so.

   a.   Note that each task was a nine-pair list, with nine different cards and three different responses. Which of the girls had positive transfer from Task I to Task II, and which had negative transfer?

   b.   Offer a coherent account of the difference between the children's performances on the second task.

5.   In 1860 divorces were very rare and people had strong convictions that marriage was permanent and forever. The average age of couples marrying for the first time was twenty-six. In 1960 divorce is very common and most young people

believe that if a marriage doesn't work out (becomes boring) they can simply be divorced and find someone new. The expectation is close to serial polygamy, and the average age of couples marrying for the first time is twenty-one.

a. Can you formulate a simple model to explain the change in age at first marriage?

b. Religious groups have different attitudes toward marriage. Catholics have stronger convictions about the permanence of marriage and make divorce more difficult than Protestants. Which group would you expect to marry younger? Why?

Diffusion

One major social phenomenon is the way in which individuals within a society modify their knowledge, behavior, practices, or beliefs over time. It is frequently interesting to consider those changes as resulting from some kind of diffusion process through the society. Thus, we often talk about the spread of a fashion. In this section of the course we consider some simple models for such phenomena.

PROBLEM SET 14

1. Herman Smith is engaged. The big event took place at 11:00 P.M., Sunday. News of the engagement first reached the women's residence halls at Irvine Tech at 11:30 P.M., when Herman called Patience Fitzpatrick to tell her he could not make it to her place that night. There are six women at Irvine Tech (including Miss Fitzpatrick but not including Mr. Smith's fiancée). Suppose that each day (between noon and one o'clock in the afternoon) these people pair off at random

and exchange current gossip. Suppose further that the news about an engagement is not particularly important; anyone who hears the news for the first time one day will pass it on to her gossip-partner of the next day but will thereafter not view it as "current."

    a.   What is the earliest morning by which all six women could know the news?

    b.   How many of I.T.'s coeds will have heard the news by the morning of Monday? Tuesday? Wednesday? Thursday? Friday? Saturday?

    c.   Is it possible that at least one of the six women will never hear the news? If so, how likely is it?

  2.   What would your answers to part 1 be if:

    a.   Herman Smith called one of the six women (at random) each day to tell her the news? Assume he called in the morning and started on Monday.

    b.   Miss Fitzpatrick never tired of repeating the news to whomever she was speaking?

  3.   What would be the effect on the rate of diffusion if:

    a.   Twice as many people had the information initially?

    b.   Each person talked to twice as many people each day (i.e., there were two gossip periods each day)?

    c.   Each person talked twice as long about the subject (i.e., she repeated the news for two days after she first heard the news?

  4.   How would you solve the problem if there were 500 women at Irvine Tech?

  5.   Consider the problem described in part 1 above:

    a.   What are the key assumptions about human behavior?

    b.   Specify one important modification you think would

make the model more realistic as a description of
the diffusion of information.

c. What makes your modification more realistic?

d. Show how your modification would change the predictions.

PROBLEM SET 15

1. Suppose that divorce in a society spreads in the following ways:

Any couple in which both sets of parents were never divorced is very unlikely ($p=0$) to seek a divorce.

Any couple in which one set of parents was divorced is
somewhat more likely ($p=.1$) to seek a divorce.

Any couple in which both sets of parents were divorced
is much more likely ($p=1$) to seek a divorce.

a. If you assume that interest in marriage and marital
choice are independent of parental divorce, that
never-divorced parents have (on the average) the
the same number of children that divorced parents
do, and that "initially" (i.e., about 1860) approximately 5 per cent of all first marriages ended in divorce, what will be the rate and pattern of divorce
in this society over time?

b. What differences would you expect in part a if you
assumed that children of divorced parents were
more likely to marry other children of divorced parents?

c. What differences would you expect in part b if you
assumed that the more children a couple has, the
less likely they are to seek a divorce?

d. If these models were correct and we wished to inhibit divorce in the society, what social action

should we take? Show what difference it would make.

e. Comment on the validity of the models, using data wherever possible. If you suggest modifications, discuss the implications of the modifications.

2. The Happy Hour Liquor Store wishes to advertise its weekend special to the Greater Irvine metropolis. The store wishes to maximize the number of people who know about the special. It has been offered three alternative "packages" by the advertising agency. In each case, the plan is to make ten spot announcements from a single radio station.

KULT is a radio station specializing in classical music and book reviews. It has a small, distinguished, and loyal audience.

KICK is an all-request rock station. It has a relatively large, loyal, and hip audience.

KROK is an all-news station. It has a relatively large audience consisting almost entirely of people riding on short trips in automobiles.

a. What kind of model would you use to evaluate these alternatives?

b. Which alternative would you recommend? Why?

c. Under what circumstances should Happy Hour consider a few spot announcements on each station instead of the concentration on a single station?

3. Take a map of a city you know well. Locate a major intersection. Assume that fifty people collapse and die from smog at that intersection between 4:50 P.M. and 5:00 P.M., Monday.

a. Predict the diffusion of information about the disaster by showing the densities of knowledge (i.e., the proportion of people in a given area who have the information) in various parts of the city at 5:30 P.M., 6:00 P.M., and 6:30 P.M.

b. Would your answer be different if the disaster occurred on Sunday?

4. Comment on each of the following statements. For each one indicate why it might be true and under what conditions it would not be true:

a. "There are no moderate successes in our business. Either you sell a hundred or you sell a million, nothing in between."

b. "The breakdown of the extended family, the increased residential mobility of Americans, and the advent of the automobile culture all combine to increase substantially the impact of mass media on political attitudes in the United States."

PROBLEM SET 16

1. The Irvine Academy, a high prestige finishing school for ladies of excellent blood but average genes, wishes to develop those qualities of good breeding and moral reliability that are the hallmark of Academy girls. Academy consultants have suggested three alternative tactics:

Segregate the ladies from contact with noxious people and ideas.

Expose the ladies deliberately to bad thoughts and people; but do it in small, well-spaced doses.

Expose the ladies deliberately to bad things in large doses, but punish them whenever they imitate such behavior.

The trustees wish to adopt the tactic with the best prospects of success in the terms above. Prepare a recommendation for them outlining a model and showing the circumstances under which each alternative would be best.

2.   Herman Smith has been drafted and is in Vietnam as an infantry squad leader. Next week his squad is scheduled to go into action for the first time. He has sent his men into Saigon for a last weekend of cultural activities while he considers the following problem:

> His troops are green. Since he is scared witless, he supposes they probably are. For the good of the whole group it is important to avoid a panic reaction to the first sight of blood.

What steps can he take (or might have taken with more time) to minimize such possibilities?

3.   For each of the following, discuss three things: First, what special problems are there in applying a diffusion model to the situation? Second, what kinds of predictions can you make from such a model? Third, how would you use the model to make recommendations for dealing with the problem and what recommendations would you make?
   a.   Diffusion of crime
   b.   Diffusion of low morale
   c.   Diffusions of accidents

Notes on Contributors

W. Ross Ashby is professor of electrical engineering at the University of Illinois. Formerly director of Burden Neurological Institute in Bristol, England, he is the author of *Design for a Brain* and *An Introduction to Cybernetics*.

C. West Churchman is professor of business administration at the University of California, Berkeley. Formerly professor of philosophy at the University of Pennsylvania, he is the author of *Theory of Experimental Inference, Methods of Inquiry,* and *Predication and Optimal Decision*.

Harold Guetzkow is professor of political science and psychology at Northwestern University. Formerly professor of industrial administration at the Carnegie Institute of Technology, he is the author of *Simulation in Social Science, Simulation in International Relations,* and *A Social Psychology for Group Processes for Decision Making*.

R. Duncan Luce is professor of psychology at the Institute for Advanced Study, Princeton University. Formerly lecturer in psychology at Harvard University, he is the author of *Individual Choice Behavior, Handbook of Mathematical Psychology,* and *Readings in Mathematical Psychology*.

James G. March is professor of psychology and sociology

and dean of the social sciences at the University of California, Irvine. Formerly professor of industrial administration at the Carnegie Institute of Technology, he is the author of *Organizations, A Behavioral Theory of the Firm,* and *Handbook of Organizations.*

William T. Morris is professor of industrial engineering at the Ohio State University. Having formerly directed research in the Air Force and in industry, he is the author of *Management Science in Action, Decentralization in Management Systems,* and *Management Science: A Bayesian Integration.*

Ralph M. Stogdill is professor of management sciences and director of the Program for Research in Leadership and Organization at the Ohio State University. Formerly associate director of the Ohio State Leadership Studies, he is the author of *Leadership and Structures of Personal Interaction, Individual Behavior and Group Achievement,* and *Managers, Employees, Organizations.*

Index